SHAMBHALA
CLASSICS

Appreciate

THE ESSENCE

EDITED BY
Wendy Egyoku Nakao
AND Eve Myonen Marko

FOREWORD BY
Bernie Glassman

YOUR LIFE

OF ZEN PRACTICE

Taizan Maezumi

SHAMBHALA
Boston & London   2002

Shambhala Publications, Inc.
Horticultural Hall
300 Massachusetts Avenue
Boston, Massachusetts 02115
www.shambhala.com

9 8 7 6 5 4 3 2 1

Printed in the United States of America
⊗ This edition is printed on acid-free paper that meets the
American National Standards Institute z39.48 Standard.
Distributed in the United States by Random House, Inc.,
and in Canada by Random House of Canada Ltd

The Library of Congress catalogues the hardcover edition as:
Maezumi, Hakuyu Taizan.
Appreciate your life: the essence of Zen practice / Taizan
Maezumi; edited by Wendy Egyoku Nakao and Eve Myonen
Marko; foreword by Bernie Glassman.—1st ed.
p. cm.
Includes bibliographical references and index.
1. Spiritual life—Zen buddhism.   I. Nakao, Wendy Egyoku.
II. Marko, Eve Myonen.   III. Title.
ISBN 1-57062-228-0 (hardcover)
ISBN 1-57062-916-1 (paperback)
BQ9288.M3   2001
294.3'444—dc21
00-046358

PHOTO CREDITS
Emmett Ho, cover
Zen Center of Los Angeles, page xvi
Jim Whiteside, page 44
Zen Center of Los Angeles, page 84

Contents

Foreword   vii

Preface   xiii

PART ONE

The Essence of Zen

Appreciate Your Life   3

Endowed from the Start   7

Three "Pillows" of Zen   13

The Dharma Seals   17

Why Zazen?   19

Do It Over and Over and Over   22

Close the Gap between Yourself and Yourself   26

The Answer Is Simple   29

Your Zazen Is the Zazen of the Buddhas   33

Practice the Paramitas   35

On Ceremonial Action   40

PART TWO

Clarify the Great Matter

What Is Koan?   47
Koan and Shikantaza   49
Raise the Bodhi Mind   54
Realize Your Life as Koan   57
Pain, Fear, and Frustration   60
Intimacy of Relative and Absolute   63
Clarify the Great Matter   67
Save All Sentient Beings   70
Koans of Zazen   74
Pure in Heart   78
Copying Sutras   81

PART THREE

Where Is the Hindrance?

Where Is the Hindrance?   87
See the Shadow of the Whip   90
The Seven Wise Sisters   94
Live the Life of Impermanence   98
Diversity and the "Right Way"   104
Thusness   106
On Becoming a Buddhist   110
On Life and Death   112
Blossoms of Nirvana   117
Unknown Life and Death   119
Shakyamuni Buddha and I Are Practicing Together   122

Appendix   125
Glossary   137
Bibliography   143

FOREWORD

I LIKE TO TELL THE STORY of how I met my teacher, Hakuyu Taizan Maezumi, for the first time. In 1963, after several years of sitting meditation on my own, I wanted to sit with a group, maybe even find a teacher. So I went to the only place I knew of in Los Angeles that had sitting meditation, which was Zenshuji, the Soto Zen temple in Little Tokyo and home to the Soto Zen bishop for North America. The temple served the needs of the Japanese-American Buddhist community by holding Zen Buddhist services, particularly funeral services. It also had a sitting group made up mostly of Caucasian Americans like myself.

One day our group did a *zazenkai,* or a one-day retreat. I noted that the abbot of the temple, who hardly spoke English, was attended by a young Japanese monk. At the end of the day we all drank tea together, and at that time I asked the abbot why we did *kinhin,* or walking meditation, between periods of *zazen,* sitting meditation. Instead of answering, he motioned to his young attendant, who said simply, "When we walk, we just walk."

The young attendant was Taizan Maezumi, and those were his first words to me. Those were also his last words to me for about five years, for I didn't return to Zenshuji. Less than twenty years had passed since the time of the internment of Japanese Americans during World War II, and some of us Caucasian Americans who were interested in sitting meditation found less than a warm welcome when we entered Japanese-American temples. Cultures and memories clashed. Purposes, too. For most Japanese Americans, Buddhism meant what Western religions mean to most Westerners who attend church or synagogue: ritual, the celebration of individual and family milestones, the pulling together of a community. We Caucasians, on the other hand, came for different reasons. Some of us came because we'd heard about meditation, others because we'd heard about enlightenment. We had very little interest in new forms of liturgy or ritual, not to mention that these were in Japanese, which we didn't understand. So I didn't go back to Zenshuji and returned to sitting on my own.

A few years later, however, I met this same young Japanese monk again. By now he was leading his own sitting group, so I went to sit with him. Right away I knew that I wished to study with him. Shortly thereafter the group moved to Normandie Avenue, and that was the beginning of the Zen Center of Los Angeles.

Maezumi Roshi came from a family prominent in the Soto Zen sect of Japan. His father, Baian Hakujun Kuroda, served as head of the Soto sect's supreme court. Kuroda Roshi was expansive and enterprising, taking a lively interest in everything around him. Like most Japanese, the Kuroda family was impoverished after World War II. Maezumi Roshi later remembered that in those days they caught cicadas for food. Nevertheless, Kuroda Roshi built the family temple despite having no money and no resources. Unlike most Soto Zen priests, he had a lot of close friendships with Buddhist priests and teachers outside the Soto sect and headed Japan's Pan-Buddhist movement. In fact, one of his good friends was Koryu Osaka Roshi, a Rinzai lay teacher who taught several of the Kuroda sons.

Maezumi Roshi took the name of his mother's family, for she had no brothers to keep her family name going; hence the name Maezumi rather than Kuroda. He received dharma transmission from his father, Kuroda Roshi, when he was twenty-four and then went to stay at Koryu Roshi's *dojo*, or practice center, and studied with him while taking classes at the Soto sect's Komazawa University. But he didn't finish his studies with Koryu Roshi at that time. Instead, he was sent in 1956 to the United States by Soto headquarters, at the age of twenty-five, to serve as a priest in Zenshuji. In addition, however, he also proceeded to continue his koan study with Nyogen Senzaki Roshi, a Rinzai teacher, which did not make the parochial Soto establishment happy back home. Since Senzaki's death, Maezumi and his students have conducted services at his grave every New Year's Day.

Zen Center of Los Angeles, referred to as ZCLA, grew quickly even while Roshi was still pursuing his studies. In the mid-1960s Hakuun Yasutani Roshi, a Soto priest and teacher, began to give teachings in the continental United States. Eido Roshi usually worked as his translator, but Maezumi was asked to help whenever Yasutani visited the West Coast. Maezumi asked Yasutani if he could study with him, and the latter agreed. They met each time Yasutani Roshi came to the United States, and did koan study together. In 1968, knowing that Yasutani Roshi was not going to return to this country, Roshi asked me to take over ZCLA for one year so that he could return to Japan and finish his studies with Yasutani Roshi, which he did, receiving *inka* (the final seal of approval) from Yasutani Roshi.

At about that same time, Maezumi received a letter from Koryu Osaka Roshi, his Rinzai teacher from years back, offering to come to the United States so that his disciple could complete the studies they had begun in the early 1950s. Koryu Roshi came to ZCLA in June 1970, and eventually Maezumi finished koan study with him and received inka from him as well. He thus received authorization to teach from three different teachers in three different Zen lineages: his father's and Yasutani Roshi's lineages (both Soto), and Koryu Roshi's lineage (Rinzai). This is highly unusual for a Japanese Zen teacher. Many study with a variety of teachers in different lineages, but very few complete their studies with all of their teachers and receive authorization to teach.

Maezumi Roshi, of course, had to finish koan study in two very different koan systems. Not only were many of the koans different from one system to another, but the order of studying them and the method and approach used were also quite different. Throughout the time that he was completing his koan studies, Roshi would not teach even beginning koans to his students. He maintained this policy even during the last stages of his studies, when he had already worked on more koans than practically any other teacher in this country.

Generally, Soto Zen teachers do not do koan study; it is considered by many a Rinzai practice. But some prominent Soto Zen teachers, like Daiun Harada Roshi and Yasutani Roshi, integrated koan study into their teaching, and so did Maezumi Roshi, also a Soto Zen teacher.

Maezumi Roshi was an important member of that early small group of Zen masters, including Shunryu Suzuki and Seung Sahn, who arrived from the East to settle in this country and founded practice centers that then spread not just in America but throughout the Western world. Their role was a critical one. The writings of D. T. Suzuki describing Zen practice were widely read by the time these Zen masters came to the West, but there were almost no *zendos* or actual practice environments when they began to teach.

Maezumi Roshi himself built two practice centers, the Zen Center of Los Angeles in downtown Los Angeles and the more monastic Zen Mountain Center in the San Jacinto Mountains near Idyllwild. From the beginning, however, his vision called for a large network of Zen centers transmitting the teachings throughout the West. For this purpose he had hundreds of students and easily a few thousand more who came into some contact with him. When he died at the age of sixty-four in 1995, he had twelve successors. As of this date there are at least thirty-five Zen centers and more than a hundred Zen groups in almost a dozen countries associated with the lineage he created, the White Plum Sangha, named after the white plum tree his father, Baian Hakujun Kuroda, loved so well.

But the breadth of one teacher's lineage doesn't tell us everything. It doesn't tell us about the challenges he and others met in transmitting the teachings from one vastly different culture to another. Nowadays, with practice centers sprouting up not only in major cities but also in

America's hinterlands, each with its own style and flavor, it's easy to underestimate and even misunderstand the achievements of these Zen pioneers. Bringing spiritual teachings that were strongly grounded in Japanese social and cultural customs to an American environment was complex and full of hurdles.

With me as well as with his other successors, Maezumi Roshi was crystal clear in his approach to this importing of Zen teachings from East to West. "Taste as much of this as you can," he told us. "Swallow what you need and spit out the rest." He was better aware than anyone of the difference in cultural contexts and that certain mores which made sense in Japan could not pass muster in the West. Already during his lifetime he witnessed his successors experiment with new forms and practices that he probably never dreamed of seeing in a Zen center.

In dharma transmission ceremonies, the teacher vows to support the successor in all of his or her teaching endeavors. My teacher stuck to his word. He supported us in all our efforts and experiments; he never once asked us to teach like him or restrict ourselves only to the forms that he had created. In my experience this is unusual, for I've known a number of Buddhist teachers from different traditions and denominations who have encountered resistance and discouragement from their Eastern teachers when they tried new forms and practices.

Maezumi Roshi died suddenly in May 1995 while on a visit to Tokyo. His death was unexpected and the transition was difficult. We grieved for him; he was only sixty-four. At the same time, I intuitively felt that he had finally passed on because he had done what he had set out to do. He had brought the Buddha dharma to the West and seen it take root. He knew better than anyone else that if it was to flower, it would have to chart out new courses and develop in new ways. He would not be the one to do that, he said, for he was Japanese.

I was his first dharma successor, receiving transmission from him in 1976. Several months after that I was giving interviews during the dawn sitting period. I rang the bell to end one interview. The student left, the door opened, and in came my teacher, Maezumi Roshi. He bowed deeply to me, sat down, and said: "My name is Taizan Maezumi. My practice is shikantaza [just-sitting]. Can you tell me how to do shikantaza?"

I told him. We had a short conversation, and when the interview was done I rang the bell. He got up, made his bows, and left the room.

As he said to his students again and again, and as he says in this book: "*Your* life is the 'treasury of the true dharma eye and subtle mind of peace.' " Your life is the life of the Buddha. Here, in this country. Right now.

Bernie Glassman
La Honda, California

PREFACE

DURING HIS LIFE AS A ZEN MASTER, Maezumi Roshi gave more than fifteen hundred *teisho*. A *teisho* is a presentation to the disciples of a master's direct realization. It is not a dharma talk or lecture, not an explanation of things-as-they-are, but a direct expression of it, a direct appeal to the true nature of the student. It was often a challenge to penetrate Maezumi Roshi's teisho. I could point to a number of factors to explain why this was so, such as the fact that he was not a native English speaker, or the cultural gap between East and West, or his use of words and concepts unfamiliar to us. But none of these reasons is as important as the fact that our true nature is for each of us subtle and difficult to realize.

Maezumi Roshi was unshakeable in his faith in his students and their capacities to realize this truth, each in their own place and time. He did not adjust his teisho to our level of understanding. Rather, he kept unveiling this nature, insisting we stretch far beyond our self-imposed limitations and plunge into the vast universe of truth.

These teisho were delivered in a specific place and time, but are not limited to them. And yet as Maezumi Roshi unrelentingly points out, place and time are nothing but this universal truth, even as they exist right now for you holding this book. He implored us to realize and appreciate our life as this. He challenged us with questions and insisted that we confirm the Buddha Way for ourselves.

The way to read this book is to eat it one bite at a time. This sampling of his teisho are best heard with one's whole being. Maezumi Roshi's teisho were not delivered in a theoretical or linear style. Rather his style—spontaneous, organic, and flowing—appealed to the experience of his students. He moved freely from one theme to another, engaging us to realize ourselves as the Way.

These teisho are not ordinary lectures, but are intimate communications from master to student. They were invariably preceded by at least one or more periods of zazen and not infrequently, were given during the course of a three- to seven-day *sesshin*. Maezumi Roshi was speaking to an audience of people in an unusual state of mind, unusually focused and attentive. So also must we realize that these same qualities were at an even more heightened level in Maezumi Roshi himself. During a *teisho*, he would sometimes shout energetically the points he wished to emphasize, he frequently quoted Dogen Zenji's writings from memory and freely translated them, and he was silent for periods of time. The effect on the listener was to merge with Maezumi Roshi's presence and to open to the intimacy of dharma.

One of the many challenges of editing these teisho was Maezumi Roshi's frequent and spontaneous recitation in Japanese of Dogen Zenji's writings. Sometimes he would use a published English translation, sometimes he reinterpreted an existing translation, and sometimes he translated on the spot. We have noted where he used previously published translations, but for the most part the versions of Dogen are Maezumi Roshi's translations. Because he was so saturated in Dogen Zenji's thought and because of the frequent and spontaneous references to Dogen's work, many of his references remain untraceable.

The project of transcribing and assembling these teisho was begun soon after Maezumi Roshi's passing. I wish to acknowledge all those who transcribed his teisho over the years and the support of the project by the White Plum Sangha and especially by the *sangha*, or community, of the Zen Center of Los Angeles. While I was working on the manuscript, Roshi Bernie Glassman asked me to return to the Zen Center of Los Angeles to take on the task of caring for Maezumi Roshi's home temple and sangha. At that point I gave the project over to Roshi Glassman and Sensei Eve Myonen Marko. In the end, she and I brought this book to completion. I express my deepest appreciation to Burt Wetanson and John Daishin Buksbazen for their careful reading of the manuscript and especially to Roshi Glassman and Sensei Eve Marko, whose collaboration made this book possible.

In reading this book, may Maezumi Roshi's realization and love of dharma permeate your being.

Wendy Egyoku Nakao
ZEN CENTER OF LOS ANGELES
LOS ANGELES, CALIFORNIA

PART ONE

The Essence of Zen

APPRECIATE YOUR LIFE

NO ONE CAN LIVE YOUR LIFE except you. No one can live my life except me. You are responsible. I am responsible. But what is our life? What is our death?

In Soto Zen we have the expression "the treasury of the true dharma eye and subtle mind of nirvana."* This expression comes from a famous koan which relates the transmission of the dharma from our original teacher, Shakyamuni Buddha, to his successor, Mahakashyapa. In the story, Shakyamuni Buddha held up a flower and blinked. Mahakashyapa smiled, and Shakyamuni Buddha said, "I have the treasury of the true dharma eye and subtle mind of nirvana, and I transmit it to Mahakash-yapa."

What is this treasury of the true dharma eye and subtle mind of nirvana that Shakyamuni Buddha transmitted? All the Buddhist teachings deal with this most precious treasure. It is your life. It is my life.

---

*In Japanese, *shobogenzo nehan myoshin*. The treasury of the true dharma eye (*shobogenzo*) and subtle mind (*myoshin*) of nirvana (*nehan*).—Eds.

Another way of asking that question is, "Who am I?" "What is this?"

These inquiries are the fundamental, most important koans. Like all koans, we must answer them out of our own life. What *is* our life? And knowing what it is, *how* are we living it? How can we experience the life that we are living now as an infinite, literally limitless life, as the subtle mind of nirvana? For the irony is that we are all living such a life, we are all living this treasure, and we are also not quite living it, either. In other words, our life is no other than the treasury of the true dharma eye and subtle mind of nirvana, and yet we see it as something other than this.

We do not see that our life right here, right now, is nirvana. Maybe we think that nirvana is a place where there are no problems, no more delusions. Maybe we think nirvana is something very beautiful, something unattainable. We always think that nirvana is something very different from our own life. But we must really understand that nirvana is right here, right now.

How is that possible? We can say that our practice is to close the gap between what we *think* our life is and our actual life as the subtle mind of nirvana. Or more to the point, how can we realize that there is really no gap to begin with?

Do not be dualistic. Truly be one with your life as the subtle mind of nirvana. That is what *subtle* means. Something is subtle not because it is hidden, nor because it is elusive, but because it is right here. We don't see it precisely because it is right in front of us. In fact, we are living it. When we live it we don't think about it. The minute we think about it, we are functioning in the dualistic state and don't see what our life is.

Why is this so difficult to do? Pin down what the difficulty is and where it comes up. Most of us know that this *I* is somehow blocking us. *I* am the one who does not see my life as the subtle mind of nirvana. *I* am the one who is not experiencing life as treasure.

What is this *I* that is blocking this realization? It is my dualistic functioning. There is nothing wrong with duality itself, that is how our mind functions. But as long as we remain in the confinement of duality, we are swayed by such opposing values as right and wrong, good and bad. These are only temporary aspects. Something appears sometimes to be good or bad or right or wrong or long or short or big or small—but what is it overall? The same thing with our life. We must see what it is beyond duality. Our life literally comes down to right now. Now! Here! What is it?

One understanding of life and death is the life and death of the instant. According to Dogen Zenji, the founder of Japanese Soto Zen, Shakyamuni Buddha said that in twenty-four hours our life is born and dying, rising and falling, 6,400,099,980 times. So in one second, our life is born and dies around seventy thousand times. Our conscious mind cannot even imagine such an occurrence. What kind of life is this?

We usually think of our life as fifty years, sixty years, maybe the most around one hundred years. I once read that there are about thirty-three hundred people who are more than one hundred years old, the oldest being 112 years. (What are people doing living such long lives?) Dogen Zenji said that living a long life without awareness is almost a crime. On the contrary, he emphasized that even if you live *one day* with a clear understanding of what life is, the value of that one day is equal to many, many years of living without awareness. We are all so concerned with how long we will live. We feel that living eighty, ninety, or a hundred years is a wonderful life. Maybe so, but wonderful compared with what? Compared with those who die young?

We must see our life clearly. The existence of this life at this very moment, what is it? Being born and dying seventy thousand times at this very moment—what is it? Is such a life different for a man, a woman, a young person, an old person, a human being, other beings? Is such a life dualistic? Is it relative or absolute? All our usual considerations and understanding about what our life is make no sense if we are born and dying seventy thousand times in an instant.

Dogen Zenji says that because our life is *this,* we attain realization. We do not practice in order to attain realization; in fact, when we practice, we do not need to expect anything. Why not? Because everything is already here! Our life *is* this wisdom! Our practice *is* this realization. When we see our life beyond duality, beyond thinking and nonthinking, then everything is already no other than the treasury of the true dharma eye and subtle mind of nirvana! When we think in dualistic terms, our life is restricted: I am, you are, this is good, this is bad. At the same time, our life has no boundary. Since we are born and die in each moment, in each instant, our life is not limited by time and space. Everything is right here, right now!

So our life is limited when we think dualistically, and at the same time it is not limited. It does not matter whether you are a man or woman, young or old, a monk or layperson. The treasury of the true dharma eye and subtle mind of nirvana is anybody, everybody!

All of us have abundant opportunities to experience our life in this way at this very moment. How can we realize the Supreme Way manifesting as our life? For whether we realize it or not, being born and dying, renewing our life thousands of times per second, we are always living this unsurpassable life—just as we are. But how do we realize this? Just be! Just do! When we live with this awareness, we realize that there is no division between this life and the Supreme Way, no division between this life and the subtle mind of nirvana. We realize the life that has no division!

This is our life. This is our practice also. So if your practice is breathing, be one with breathing! If your practice is shikantaza, or just-sitting, then just sit! If your practice is koan, *be* the koan! Are you truly practicing in this way? If you are doing shikantaza based on a certain understanding or expectation, your practice is not shikantaza. If you are practicing with a koan intellectually or as a riddle to solve, you are not doing koan practice. Why not? Because duality is still involved! Because division is still involved.

How can you experience and confirm your life as the true dharma eye and subtle mind of nirvana? You are already so! Start at least with believing that your life is this. Have faith in this! Then experience that life as your very own! When you do this, right there your life is *prajna paramita* wisdom itself. *Prajna* is the wisdom of no duality, no I, you, good, or bad. It is the functioning of this moment, of what happens here and now. *Paramita* means "to have reached the other shore." What other shore? If everything is right here and now, what other shore exists? Some people think that the other shore is nirvana, the way we think things should be, the way we wish our life to be. But nirvana is already here. Having reached the other shore, we confirm that this life right now *is* nirvana. This life is that most precious treasure, the unsurpassable Way, the way of true realization.

Shakyamuni Buddha himself lived this life. What is the difference between his life and our life? At the moment of his great enlightenment, Shakyamuni Buddha said, "How miraculous! All beings have the wisdom and virtue of the Tathagata Buddha!" Shakyamuni Buddha's confirmation of who we are, of what our life is, and of how to live is *our* koan. We must live it and practice it. Do you understand this?

Each of us has to take care of this treasury of the true dharma eye and subtle mind of nirvana. We must do it. One day is long enough. One sitting period is long enough. Even one second is long enough. And vice versa. A week, ten years, fifty years, or a hundred years may not be long enough. In order to experience yourself in this way, you do not need to wait for any moment. In fact, do not wait!

I encourage you. Please enjoy this wonderful life together. Appreciate the world of *just this!* There is nothing extra. Genuinely appreciate your life as the most precious treasure and take good care of it.

ENDOWED FROM THE START

How should we sit properly? Zazen, or sitting meditation, should be physically comfortable. At the same time, zazen is the practice and realization of manifesting our body as *bodhi,* as enlightenment. It is both the practice and the realization, for when we truly do zazen, there is no distinction between practice and realization. It is wisdom *as is,* as things are. This zazen, the practice of the Buddha Way, is none other than the practice of one's life.

The best way to practice is to forget the self. By forgetting the self, we can appreciate our life not in the narrow, restricted, isolated way that we usually live but rather as a life of unity, a life that is unsurpassable. Another way to explain what we mean by forgetting the self is that we are transcending the subject-object relationship or the I-Other relationship. We are transcending duality.

So how can each of us really do the best zazen?

Our physical and mental postures are very important. The position of the hands, or mudra, symbolizes the unity of opposites. It reflects a sense of harmony, a kind of completeness or perfection. In the Soto school we have a special mudra of Maha Vairochana Buddha, the manifestation of formless forms.

There are two ways to form Vairochana's mudra. According to both Keizan Zenji and Dogen Zenji, the founders of Soto Zen, place your left hand on the right palm. There are different explanations for this. For instance, we say the right hand is the hand of yang, active, and the left hand is yin, quiet or passive. So when we do zazen we put the left hand on the right hand so that the less active left hand calms the active right hand, the activity of the body and mind. But when you see the statue of Maha Vairochana Buddha, the right hand is on the left palm, so there are two ways of forming this mudra.

The tips of the thumbs, lightly touching, are held evenly in a horizontal position. Some people tilt their hands without realizing it. Hold your hands like the surface of still water, calm and without tension. Sitting too tensely or too loosely is reflected in your mudra. If your thumbs are pressed tightly and rigidly together, or if your hands are apart and the thumbs don't meet, all these tell you something about your sitting. When sitting in the half lotus position,* your hands may rest on your foot. Let the mudra be well balanced. Even though you think that you are sitting correctly, it is not so simple to keep the mudra in the right position. It is very helpful to sit in front of a mirror and check your posture, or have someone check your posture for you.

It is also important to pay attention to our feet. When we sit in the half lotus or in the full lotus position, the tops of our feet rest on our

* To sit in the half lotus position, place the right foot under the left thigh, then place the left foot over the right thigh.—Eds.

thighs. I understand that there are about seven hundred acupuncture points and about sixteen meridians, all relating to one particular point in the sole. In putting the feet in the half or the full lotus position, the soles are nicely stimulated. The body settles down and we can physically sit very comfortably.

When you sit on a chair, be aware of these principles and place the soles of your feet firmly on the floor. The soles of the feet are like the roots of a tree. The roots are growing, penetrating into the ground—not necessarily pushing their way into the earth but naturally filling it. Have your body in the same way, solid and penetrating into the ground. We become strong by doing so, and we can sense the unity and harmony with the earth.

When you have settled your body, sway your upper body from side to side in large arcs, slowly decreasing the angle of swaying. As you decrease the angle of swaying, adjust your spine so that it is upright and let it settle in this upright position. Tuck in your chin and let your eyes settle half open, setting your gaze about three to four feet in front of you at a forty-five degree angle. Then start sitting. When you come out of zazen, sway your body again, but in reverse. Slowly start swaying in small arcs, increasing to large arcs. Sway not only your body but also your concentration, so that you can carry that concentration into standing and walking. This slow swaying is a very natural procedure. When your *samadhi* is strong, you can't immediately jump up from sitting. Standing very quickly indicates your samadhi is not very strong. Easing the body into and out of the sitting posture can help you focus your concentration.

When you are settled for zazen, take several deep breaths. In English we say inhale and exhale. In Japanese we say *kokyu*. *Ko* is exhalation and *kyu* is inhalation. It may seem more logical for your inhalation to come first, but after settling your body, exhale first. When you exhale, exhale as much air as possible through your mouth, not your nostrils. Our exhalations are usually very small, so open your mouth slightly and exhale completely so that you feel your lungs are squeezed. You can bend slightly forward when exhaling.

When you exhale through the mouth, you have a direct sensation of exhaling toxins from the body, not just breathing out air. Then when you have to inhale, the air comes in quickly. Expand your lungs to breathe deeply. Then once again, exhale and inhale in the same way. While exhaling, you can squeeze and tighten the muscles in your butt, relaxing when you inhale. Then let your breathing return to normal. Let your breathing become relaxed.

Regarding breathing, I am reminded of one of my teacher Koryu Roshi's favorite expressions. He said that when you breathe in, swallow the whole universe. When you breathe out, breathe out the whole universe. In and out. In and out. Eventually you forget about the division between breathing in and breathing out; even breathing is totally forgotten. You just sit with a sense of unity.

We put our mental concentration in the *hara*. The *hara* is a point in our body that generates *chi*, energy, and it is approximately two inches below the navel. If we sit in half or full lotus position and the soles of our feet are supported by our thighs, they are close to the hara and receive more stimulation from our concentration, and altogether the entire body functions better.

Having settled our body and breath, we next adjust the mind. In his *Universal Promotion of the Principles of Zazen (Fukanzazengi)*, Dogen Zenji writes, "Think of not-thinking. How do you think of not-thinking? Non-thinking. This in itself is the essential art of zazen."* In other words, penetrate into one point, into the nondual state.

When we sit, we may have the experience of observing. Observing includes the observer and the object that is being observed. This is dualistic. As long as we are dualistic, we can't experience being, seeing, hearing, smelling, touching. As long as there is a division between you and something else, there is a separation. You can make a conscious effort of seventy, eighty or even up to ninety percent to eliminate this gap. But as long as you are consciously trying and holding an object, you can't quite do it. The very last ten percent is the most important effort.

---

* Norman Waddell and Masao Abe, trans., "Fukanzazengi (The Universal Promotion of the Principles of Zazen) by Dogen Zenji," in *On Zen Practice II: Body, Breath and Mind,* ed. Hakuyu Taizan Maezumi and Bernard Tetsugen Glassman (Los Angeles: Zen Center of Los Angeles, 1976), 14.

The way to realize yourself one hundred percent is to penetrate into samadhi, the state of nonthinking. As long as we remain within the confines of the thinking mind, we can't experience the state of non-thinking. If we can't experience nonthinking, we will not understand what our life truly is. Please realize this for yourself. Just sit!

Just-sitting is perhaps the most difficult thing to do. For in order to just-sit, we have to forget the self. What does that mean? There are no thoughts because there is no thinker. Instead, we *are* the thoughts that come up. There are no bird songs because there are no concepts of bird songs. Instead, we *are* those sounds. In the same way we are the rain-drops, we are the thunder and the lightning. In sitting, the whole uni-verse is revealed and manifested.

In zazen we do not expect anything. Zazen is not a technique to achieve anything, it is much more natural. And yet, somehow the most natural thing is difficult to do. How come? Because we think. There is nothing wrong with thinking. Thinking is a very natural process, but we are so easily conditioned by our thinking and give too much value to it. We try to take care of ourselves, of our ego structures, by thinking. Thinking is an abstraction. It is not being, it is thinking about being. And since we are born and die seven thousand times in one second, the conditions that we think about are already gone. We are thinking about shadows rather than being this very life itself.

A famous koan states that mind is ungraspable. Since mind and body are not two, this body is ungraspable. And yet there is a way to appreci-ate the ungraspable. How? By *being* it. The whole, complete being mani-festing *as is*. Everything is here right now. Nirvana is right here. But somehow we ignore that fact, and we start doing something else or looking for something else. All these expectations are unnecessary. There is no need to look for any further accomplishment or attainment of anything. Everything is already here.

Zazen is our life, the life of the Buddha Way, the way to practice the Buddha dharma. Dogen Zenji wrote: "To study the Buddha Way is to study the self. To study the self is to forget the self. To forget the self is to be enlightened by the ten thousand dharmas." To study this life and to forget the self mean to truly be the Way. The Way is not a path or a direction. The Way is everything. Each of us is the Way. At each moment, everything is all together liberated, manifesting as a whole. It is not one's own activity—for in zazen the one has disappeared—but the activity of all the buddhas. All phenomena of the entire universe are unified with one's own activity. This is the kind of zazen we should appreciate.

The experience of this body and mind *as is* is the plain, universal fact that all the ancient masters realized. It is the realization that the Way is complete. Everything is here. No artificial devices are needed. But the Way is difficult to realize because our conditioned mind creates a gap between Oneself and oneself. If we are always thinking, if we see our life only in dualistic terms, then we cannot forget the self. Therefore devices can sometimes be effective. Some devices are like surgical treatments, others more like herbal treatments. Removing the bad parts in surgery can be effective but sometimes drastic. Herbal treatments, on the other hand, are a more gradual process and are also effective. But even so, when we realize the Way, there is no quick and there is no gradual. How can we experience this Way?

There are many different kinds of aspects to our life and practice. I simply encourage you in one way or another to penetrate into this life and utilize any opportunity that is available. If you think it is necessary, you can try all sorts of schemes or devices. But do not forget that everything is with you to begin with. When you sit, please remind yourself how you can sit best. When you do that, all the buddhas and ancestors guarantee it is the right way. Have good trust in yourself—not in the one that you think you should be, but in the One that you are.

Three "Pillows" of Zen

WHAT IS THE PRIMARY MATTER of our practice? It always comes back to oneself, to one's own life. We say clarify yourself. Clarify the matter of your life and death. How do we do that? Dogen Zenji says, "Forget the self." Are you forgetting yourself or are you reinforcing yourself? This is very important.

What is the state of forgetting oneself? There is a book called *The Three Pillars of Zen*.* As the title indicates, there are certain foundations in Zen. When I first heard this title, I thought it was *Three Pillows of Zen*. It seems to me that *pillars* or *pillows* does not make much difference. In order to sleep comfortably, you need these three pillows. Otherwise, you will have nightmares.

The first pillow is samadhi. One common meaning of samadhi is concentration. In order to forget oneself, concentrate on one single thing. We have the simple analogy that the mind is like water in a bucket. When we move the bucket around, the water moves, too. Let the bucket sit, and the water eventually calms down. If the water is muddy, it gets cloudy when we stir it up. But leave it for a while, and the mud sinks down to the bottom and the water becomes transparent.

Sitting is sometimes compared to this, but there is one big difference between settling the body down in zazen and the muddy water settling down in the bucket. The crucial difference is our conscious mind, which functions autonomously. It moves by itself, stirring up the water and mud. So how to keep the mind transparent? By concentration. When you sit, if you let that autonomous mind go on, it goes on and on and on. It never stops. The conscious mind is comfortable that way because there is constant change, constant distraction. It is almost like watching television. Imagine that your mind is a blank television tube with all kinds of thoughts arising all the time. It can be very entertaining.

We have various schemes, such as counting the breath, to reduce the

* Philip Kapleau, *The Three Pillars of Zen: Teaching, Practice, and Enlightenment* (New York: Anchor, 1989).

numerous thoughts that bubble up. Counting the breath is one of the beginning practices for students as a way of strengthening their concentration. The practice is to count to ten. You can count your inhalation separately and your exhalation separately, or you can count both as one. The activities of your mind are reduced to ten, or maybe twenty. It is a very effective way to calm yourself down. When you do this, you raise your power of concentration.

Raising samadhi power is always gradual; no one can do it overnight. I think this is true for any kind of practice. You do the same thing over and over, just practicing the most basic thing. When I was a kid, I practiced Japanese archery. You draw the bow over and over in order to master the form. You need to learn how to pull, how much to pull, how to face the target, how to open the legs, where to hit; you need to master not only the position of the hands but also the position of the feet. So when you really become an expert, the arrow hits the target even if you close your eyes. Of course, my arrows hit emptiness!

In art, in sports, in music, in anything, we practice basic things over and over. When we do this kind of practice we become stronger, both mentally and physically. Even with all this practicing, I am still a rough man. When I was young I was crazy. My nickname was Gangster. I did not think I was a terrible boy, but people told me I was. If I had not practiced zazen I might have ended up a gangster. I feel I was saved by zazen. So focus, concentrate!

Another implication of samadhi is evenness. If our mind is even, if our mind is open, then we can accept everything that happens in the same way. We are not attached to one thing over another. If our mind is not even or open, then what we perceive will appear deformed to us. So how do we make our mind even?

A third implication of samadhi is to properly perceive externals. How can you properly perceive externals? By emptying yourself, by forgetting yourself, by forgetting your thoughts and concepts about those things you perceive as externals. In other words, have the proper relationship with externals. We often talk about everything as it is. Are we really perceiving everything as it is? If so, fine. But unfortunately, it is often not so. Even seeing the same thing, fifty of us perceive it differently.

How can we perceive properly? By making ourselves empty; by not being attached to our concepts of the things we perceive. This is the first pillow. Make yourself comfortable with this pillow.

The second pillow is to forget oneself. How does forgetting oneself happen? By raising samadhi. There are many different states of samadhi, many different levels of concentration. But one such experience or state is not a big thing. Dogen Zenji says it is like sticking your head into a gateway. Why is it so special to become aware of one's own life? Isn't it rather extraordinary that we do not realize who we are?

This life is ungraspable. Why is it ungraspable? Because life is limitless. We can understand this intellectually up to a point. But how can we fully experience this unlimited, boundless life? Simply forget the self. *Be* this life! Without exception, we are all this limitless, ungraspable, nonthinking life. This is the second pillow.

When you do zazen, simply identify yourself as zazen. How do you identify yourself with Yourself? In a sense, you are already doing this whether or not you realize this. Still, you sense a gap between your apparent self, which suffers and struggles, and your true self. Your apparent self and your true self are not separate. This is difficult to take in, isn't it? We cannot grasp this very state of existence through intellectual means. The true self rejects such human devices.

When you really grasp this fact, joy is just joy. Pain is just pain. But in the midst of joy and pain, there is no joy and there is no pain. In the midst of thinking, there is no thinking. In the midst of the self, there is no self. This is the fundamental wisdom of zazen.

The third pillow is actualization. When you forget the self, you are liberated and confirmed by all things. This is the realization of the oneness of life. You then must extend this realization into your daily life and make your life the realized life.

So mere sitting is not enough. You must reveal this wisdom in the way you live. How can we live this realization? Just living in a realized way is still not enough. We must share it together, with each other. How can we share it best with everybody, so that all of us can live the enlightened life? That is the third pillow.

These three pillows are the basics of our practice. When we carefully examine what different masters say, it may sound like they are talking about different things, but actually they are not, they are simply emphasizing different aspects of this process.

In some ways koan study can be seen as running parallel to these three pillows. Generally, we do not begin koan study unless we have mastered some level of concentration. Hakuin Zenji talks about nine different stages of koan practice, but these stages can be reduced to three. The first is to realize who you are, what your life is. This stage corresponds to samadhi, to an open, even mind that perceives externals properly. The famous koan Mu is one important koan in this group.* The next stage is to function freely. You cannot be static. Do whatever you are supposed to do freely. This corresponds to the second pillow, forgetting oneself. We act freely when we are not attached to this or that. The third stage is to further accomplish the Way, trim off all unnecessary parts of oneself. This corresponds to the third pillow, actualization. When we actualize our realization of the wholeness of life, then our daily life itself is nirvana; in fact, then words like *realization* or *actualization* are no longer necessary, for they are schemes and devices that we no longer need.

Of course, we can't just jump into this actualization. This is why our practice advances little by little, though in a sense, there is no little by little. And yet, even though we are the Way, we don't know it. Even though our life is already realized, we don't see it as such. How is our life in realization? Just as we are. Just as you are. Just as everything is. How can we appreciate our life in this way? This is a very basic issue of our practice.

* Maezumi Roshi is referring to the following koan: A monk asked Joshu, "Does a dog have Buddha nature?" Joshu replied, "*Mu* [nonbeing, negation]!"—Eds.

The Dharma Seals

Practice can be described in four steps. The first is, listen to the dharma. How do you listen? You can listen with your ears. You can also listen with your eyes, as you do with a written document. Next, reflect upon the teachings that you have heard. If you think the teachings are true, then the next step is practice. Work with the teachings. There are all kinds of teachings, and even when you practice them, the important points may not be clear to you. So the fourth step is to verify the teachings through your practice. Confirm the teachings—experience the teachings—not in your head but throughout your whole being. This is the experience of realization.

The dharma seals are impermanence, no-self, and peace. Do you understand the plain fact of impermanence? Everything is in constant change. I've already mentioned one of the teachings of the Abhidharma,* that in just one second life is changing thousands and thousands of times. In one second! Our conscious awareness simply cannot follow such rapid change. And yet we are living this life. How are we living it? What kind of things do we spend our time thinking about? The past is already gone, yet we cling to it. The future is not yet here, but we dwell on it. Even when we talk about *now,* there is no such thing. Even as we talk, the *now* we are talking about is already gone.

The life in our heads, the life we think is our life, is not our real life. Our real life is the life of everything and everyone. We constantly talk about doing this and doing that, about things already gone or yet to come. We play with our life in our heads, but this is not our real existence. We should not mix them up.

I am not devaluing thoughts. Just do not mix up what we *think* with what actually *is.* Buddha said that everything is constantly changing. Constant change *is* the real life, and is therefore unknowable. Since we also are constantly changing, each of us is also unknowable. And this un-

---

* The *Abhidharma* is a collection of doctrinal commentary on the Buddha dharma and is the earliest compilation of Buddhist philosophy and psychology.

knowable, impersonal no-self, not fixed in one way or another by any kind of values or attachments, is working perfectly. That no-self is not attached to anything, so it can work with everything. Do you understand impermanence, this no fixed thing, which is no-self? When you do not see this no-self, suffering is waiting for you. When you see that nothing is fixed, there is peace.

Impermanence is also an encouragement for our practice. When you enter practice through feeling impermanence, your practice will be stronger and you will not easily regress.

These three dharma seals are not three different things but rather one thing—your life—from three different perspectives. Sometimes a fourth dharma seal of suffering is included. This suffering is an ongoing sense that you are somehow not complete, that your life is somehow not whole. So you can appreciate your life from these perspectives and see how easily they overlap. For example: When you understand impermanence, you understand the nature of suffering and no-self. When you understand no-self, that is the peace of nirvana. The word *nirvana* is translated in different ways, such as "perfect bliss" or "extinction of all desires." But nirvana and impermanence are like front and back. When you understand impermanence, you find peace. When you truly see your life as nirvana, then impermanence is taken care of. So rather than figuring out how to deal with impermanence, consider these dharma seals all together as the dharma to be realized.

Remember the four steps of practice that we described in the beginning: listen to the teachings, reflect on them, practice them, and finally experience them in your life. Examine your practice. Refresh and encourage yourself. Realize your life as peace itself, your life as it is now. We do not need to expect anything; in a sense we do not need to try to do something about being peaceful. The reason is simple: peace is already here as your life. Isn't it fascinating? Realizing constant change and no fixed self, you yourself are peace. Then being peace, how are you living?

Why zazen?

This question was commonly asked by Dogen Zenji's students. In *Shobogenzo Bendowa,* Dogen Zenji asks eighteen questions about zazen and answers them himself. Let us look at the first three questions.

The first question is: "We have now heard that the merit of zazen is lofty and great, but an ignorant person may be doubtful and say, 'There are many gates for Buddha dharma. Why do you recommend zazen exclusively?' " The answer: "Because this is the front gate for the Buddha dharma."

Many of you have this same question. There are so many different ways to appreciate the dharma. We study the dharma. Our life itself is dharma. Even without doing zazen we can practice, we can understand, maybe we can understand even better. So why is there so much emphasis on sitting? Because it is the front gate for penetrating the teachings of the Buddha.

The second question naturally follows: "Why do you regard zazen alone as the front gate?" Dogen Zenji answers: "The great master Shakyamuni correctly transmitted this splendid method of training in the Way. The Tathagatas of past, future, and present all attained the Way by doing zazen. For this reason it has been transmitted as the front gate. Not only that, but also all ancestors in India and China have attained the Way by doing zazen. Thus, I now teach this front gate to human beings and *deva*s [gods]."

What does the Way mean? It could also be translated as enlightenment, or to enlighten. It means to gain the Way, to realize the Way, or to attain enlightenment. Dogen Zenji does not say just sit and do not expect to realize or to attain anything. Rather, he says, all buddhas and masters did zazen and attained the Way. From zazen, the Way emerges. Attainment is the natural function of zazen. So it is not a matter of do not attain enlightenment or do not seek after enlightenment. It happens! Just don't be too crazy about it happening.

Dogen Zenji says that great enlightenment is like eating meals or drinking tea. In other words, enlightenment is as common as eating or drinking. So do not go chasing crazily after it. Just do zazen and make clear what the Buddha dharma, the One Body, is. This Buddha dharma is the treasury of the true dharma eye, which is no other than the life of each of us.

The third question is longer. "We understand that you have correctly transmitted the Tathagata's excellent method and studied the tracks of the ancestors. It is beyond the reach of ordinary thought. However, reading sutras or chanting the Buddha's name of itself must be a cause of enlightenment. How can zazen, just sitting uselessly and doing nothing, be depended upon for attaining enlightenment?" Some of you might have a similar question, too.

Dogen Zenji's answer is also long, but let me quote part of it. I like this passage:

> If you think that the samadhi of all buddhas, their unsurpassable great method, is just sitting uselessly and doing nothing, you'll be one who slanders the Great Vehicle. Your delusion will be deep, like saying that there is no water when you are in the middle of the great ocean. Already, all buddhas graciously sit at ease in self-fulfilling samadhi. Is this not producing great merit? What a pity that your eyes are not yet open, that your mind is still intoxicated.
>
> Now, the realm of all buddhas is inconceivable. It can't be reached by consciousness. Much less can those who have no trust, who lack wisdom, know it. Only those who have right trust and great capacity can enter this realm. Those who have no trust will not accept it however much they are taught. Even at the assembly on Vulture Peak,* there were those who were told by Shakyamuni Buddha, "You may leave if you wish."†

* Vulture Peak refers to the location where the Buddha preached the *Lotus Sutra*.—Eds.
† Kazuaki Tanahashi, *Moon in a Dewdrop: Writings of Zen Master Dogen* (San Francisco: North Point Press, 1985), 147–148.

Studying the sutras intellectually is not quite enough. Dogen Zenji emphasizes the attaining of awareness. Zazen is not just idle sitting. If you say that is your practice, you slander the Great Vehicle.*

Dogen Zenji says, "Already all buddhas graciously sit at ease in self-fulfilling samadhi." He urges us to practice zazen correctly and actualize this self-fulfilling samadhi of all the buddhas. In Japanese, the word for self-fulfilled samadhi is *jijuyu zanmai*. *Ji* means "self," *ju* means "to receive," and *yu* means "to use." So, receive yourself and use yourself freely. What does it mean to receive and use oneself? *Zanmai* is samadhi, being this freely functioning life of the Buddhas.

Dogen Zenji talks about this in the first paragraph of *Bendowa*. Self-fulfilling samadhi is to realize the supreme wisdom that has been directly transmitted from Buddha to buddhas and ancestors. Verify this! Experience this supreme wisdom yourself as self-fulfilling samadhi, truly self-contained, truly content. This is given from buddha to buddha; there is no discrepancy there. And if you are not truly self-contained, then become that! Do zazen and close the gap between your life and the buddhas' life. With the mind of no-separation, you yourself will emerge as that self-fulfilled samadhi.

Self-fulfilled samadhi is sometimes translated as self-joyous samadhi, but it does not matter whether samadhi is joyous, overwhelming, or whatever. This samadhi is Oneself. As thorough as Oneself. It is totally autonomous. How do we enjoy this samadhi? In one way or other we are in that samadhi, regardless of whether we recognize it or not, regardless of whether we struggle with it or not. So why not enjoy it as much as we can?

There is the famous koan of Daitsu Chisho Buddha, who sat in the zendo for ten *kalpa*s, or countless ages, and the Buddha dharma never appeared. Why not? No attainment was accomplished. What does this mean? You yourself are in the same sphere, living the same life as Daitsu Chisho Buddha. For ten kalpas, you yourself have already been in this state of attainment. Regardless of how long Daitsu Chisho Buddha sits,

* Mahayana Buddhism—Eds.

regardless of how long you sit, the Buddha dharma never appears because it is already here! Reveal it! Do not cover it up!

In order to reveal it, the best practice is zazen. Dogen Zenji says, "Right trust. Right faith. Great vessel. Great capacity." Those who have great capacity can believe this, and they can enjoy it. And those who have small capacity cannot believe it. Those with small capacity say, "No, I am no good. My life cannot be the life of the Buddha." Do you say this?

Only those who have right trust and great capacity can realize that we are already this! Let it reveal itself. You do not need to bring in anything from anyplace or anybody—this is shikantaza. You and zazen merge into one—this is the Buddha!

I encourage you to have a very basic understanding of zazen and of what we are practicing. We are revealing the life of each of us as self-fulfilling samadhi, as nothing other than the alive, vital activity of all the buddhas. When we reveal this, we will see that Shakyamuni is still alive. Please encourage yourself in this way so that you fully appreciate this transient, frenzied life as the self-contained, self-fulfilled life of all the buddhas. Appreciate this as *your* life!

Do It Over and Over and Over

How do you answer when someone asks you, "Why do you practice?"

In the *Genjo Koan,* Dogen Zenji says:

To study the Buddha Way is to study the self.
To study the self is to forget the self.
To forget the self is to be enlightened by the ten thousand dharmas.

To be enlightened by the ten thousand dharmas is to free one's body and mind and those of others. *

The word *narau,* or "study," is more like "to repeat something over and over and over." We could also say "to learn," but not necessarily to learn something new. Perhaps an even better word would be *practice.* To practice the Buddha Way is to practice oneself, or just live life. This seemingly repetitive process is nothing but one's own life.

Our practice is much more than acquiring some kind of knowledge; instead, the implication of practice is doing over and over and over and over. In a way that is what we do in zazen. Of course, our zazen is not just learning something over and over; rather, as Dogen Zenji says, it is realization itself. In other words, do not separate practice and realization. We do not practice for the sake of realization; realization is already here. Each of us has some realization, one person more, one person less. When you do zazen day after day, time after time, moment after moment, you are manifesting yourself as that realization. Repeat what you know by merging your life into what you know, or what you have studied, and do this over and over and over again.

Dogen Zenji says, "To study the Buddha Way is to study oneself." How do we study ourselves? How do we practice ourselves? I say "we," but it is always singular. My life! Your life! The Buddha dharma, the One Body, is completely my life, completely your life. Shakyamuni Buddha himself found this out. That is why he said: "How wonderful! I and everyone in the universe are enlightened." Not just *I,* but everyone. That is what *I* means; *I* means everyone. But knowing this is not enough. That is why the words *learn* or *study* are not quite sufficient. They do not convey this sense of over and over and over. In other words, minute after minute, how do we live our life as the One Body, or the One Body as our life? No more, no less.

Dogen Zenji said, "To study the self is to forget the self." When the

* Eihei Dogen, "Shobogenzo Genjo Koan," trans. by Hakuyu Taizan Maezumi and Francis Cook, in *The Way of Everyday Life: Zen Master Dogen's Genjokoan with Commentary by Hakuyu Taizan Maezumi,* Los Angeles, Center Publications, 1978.

Buddha dharma and my life are separate, when I do not see that my life is the One Body, that is a delusion. When I see that they are together, that is the so-called enlightened life, or the *genjo* koan. *Genjo Koan* is the name of one of the writings of Dogen Zenji. We translate it as Manifesting Absolute Reality. In other words, absolute reality manifests as one's own life. How do we work with this koan? By realizing and living our life as the Buddha dharma, as the enlightened life. By not talking about enlightenment as if it is something outside our own life. Even talking about delusion or enlightenment is already a kind of delusion. The same can be said for studying koans or for doing shikantaza. When we set anything up as the object, as something outside ourselves, right there we are conditioned by it. It does not matter how fine the object is, the result is the same. It is a deluded view, a kind of ego trip because in one way or another the ego is involved. It is very easy to be trapped there.

How can you forget the self? Dogen Zenji says, "To forget the self is to be enlightened by the ten thousand dharmas." To be enlightened, to be confirmed, or to be verified by the ten thousand dharmas simply means to be verified by anything and everything, or more straightforwardly, by all of life itself. Life is verified by itself. It has to be! When we forget the self, all we are is the ten thousand dharmas, all we are is life itself. This is how we must live, over and over again.

"To be enlightened by ten thousand dharmas is to free one's body and mind and those of others." In other words, there is no division between oneself and others. The Buddha realized this when he saw the morning star. Seeing into his own nature, he saw the universality of his life, the freedom of his life. Life is absolutely free from the beginning. It is not at all restricted. The Buddha found this out, and we should appreciate our life in this way. When you are truly unconditionally open, you are forgetting the self at that moment. If you are hanging on to something, you have the self and you are not completely open. When we truly forget the self, there is no division between inside and outside, no division between yourself and externals. In such a way, we can appreciate life in its fullness.

I think openness is a wonderful characteristic of the American temperament. How can we be unconditionally open? What kind of openness are we talking about? Thorough openness itself is the best wisdom. When you are open, you are able to be one with another person. It does not matter if the person is a close friend or a stranger.

Some of you ask, "How do I apply this to the workaday world? I have stress-filled workdays. How can I forget the self in the midst of trying to meet deadlines?" Simply put yourself completely into your work and just do whatever needs to be done. Deadline after deadline? There is no deadline! Each moment is a beginning as well as an end, not a goal or a deadline set up by someone else.

So when you practice shikantaza, just sit. This is the condition of openness. Then, being totally open, you are nothing other than all space and time. Dogen Zenji says, "On this body, put the Buddha seal." The Buddha seal is this openness, where there is no conditioning, no division between yourself and the object, no division between yourself and your life. When you close this gap, Dogen Zenji says, you become "the Buddha seal itself; the whole space becomes subtly itself." If we are open this much, is there anything else that we need?

For the most part, we are not just sitting; we are nursing delusions one after another. There is often this feeling that *I am doing shikantaza*. When we have this feeling, then shikantaza is not at all shikantaza. Instead, there is some kind of maneuvering, some kind of action of one's self. Do not be fooled by words and ideas. When you practice with a koan, take the koan as your life. Koans are not something to study or evaluate apart from yourself. Make your life itself *genjo* koan, the realization of koan. This is what your life already *is*. Such a life is totally open and full, and one is not conscious of oneself.

So imprint the Buddha seal, not the human seal, upon your body and mind and penetrate this openness. Just do this over and over and over.

CLOSE THE GAP BETWEEN
YOURSELF AND YOURSELF

WE HAVE A PRACTICE KNOWN as the *paramitas*. *Paramita* means "to have reached the other shore." Dogen Zenji says, "The other shore is already reached." In other words, the meaning of reaching the other shore is to realize that this shore *is* the other shore. This life *is* the unsurpassable, realized life. There is no gap.

So if there is purpose to our practice, it is to realize that this shore and the other shore are the same. The purpose is to close the gap, to realize that there is just one shore, there is just one life. *To reach* is extra. Until you realize that this shore where you stand, this life that you are living, and the other shore, the life of the buddhas, are the same shore, you cannot appreciate your life to the fullest.

In that sense we can say that the purpose of practice is no purpose. If we have a purpose, then we have problems. We set up all kinds of goals and we reach for them. But the amazing thing is that the goal is right here! We are on the starting line and at the same time we are already on the goal line. In other words, we are already living the buddhas' life. Regardless of whether we realize it or not, regardless of whether we are new or old-time practitioners, we are intrinsically the buddhas. Yet until we see this, somehow we simply cannot accept that fact.

We get stuck when we try to figure this out intellectually. From the intellectual point of view, the start and the goal must be different. This shore and the other shore cannot be the same. Then what to do? There are as many different paths to realization as there are people. But we can say there are two basic ways. One way is to push ourselves to realize that our life is the buddhas' life. Another way is to simply let our life be the buddhas' life and just live it. In a way, this is the difference between koan practice and shikantaza. But whichever practice you do, the point is the same. *Do not create a gap between your life and the buddhas' life.*

How do we do this? How can we realize the other shore is here,

THE ESSENCE OF ZEN

right now? In other words, how can you become one with breathing, with koan, with zazen, with work, or with whatever you do? Do not play with intellectual comprehension. This is the biggest source of trouble. Unfortunately, we are usually not even aware that we are being intellectual. Simply by being in our heads, we become self-centered. We make others and self separate. As long as ideas are involved, regardless of how fine our ideas are, this gap is there.

So how are you practicing? When you count your breaths, just count breath after breath. Soon you will forget about counting and become the number. When you do shikantaza, just sit. When you do zazen, become zazen yourself. When you work on koan, become the koan yourself. Otherwise, regardless of how much you practice, you will not be satisfied.

The pitfall is always within yourself. Everything is already here with you! This very body and mind is the Way. You are complete to begin with. There is no gap, but you think there is.

Master Joshu asked Nansen, "What is the Way?" Nansen answered, "Ordinary mind is the Way." If you think ordinary mind is the Way, right there you miss. If you think that our ordinary mind, which is nothing but the monkey mind, cannot be the Way, you also miss. The point is your ordinary mind and the Way cannot be separate. Saying ordinary mind is the Way is not enough, for the word *is* points to separation. So how can you eliminate this separation? How can you realize that there is no separation to begin with?

The most important point is to forget yourself. What we do most of the time is exactly the opposite. We reinforce the self. Always, *I* am doing something. This is the problem; we create this separation. When you truly forget yourself, a very different scenery is revealed in front of your nose. The other shore is where you stand. The buddhas' life is your life. So please, however you have been practicing, really focus on forgetting yourself.

How to close the gap between Yourself and yourself? Please take this seriously as your fundamental koan. Sit comfortably and concentrate well. There are all kinds of things that disturb our practice. We call these disturbances makyo. Ma means "devil" and kyo is "object." So makyo is an object of the devil. Not having enough money could be makyo; having too many things could be makyo. If you are diligent, your effort could be makyo; not expending your energy in the right direction could also be makyo. When you are disturbed, your mind becomes scattered and you cannot concentrate well. Many people become sick simply because they do not know what to do with themselves.

How do we make our lives more orderly? When you stabilize your life you will concentrate better, and when you eliminate all separation you will realize the Buddha's wisdom. Upon his realization, Shakyamuni Buddha declared, "I and all beings simultaneously attained the Way." This is true order, the order of no-order. All dharma comes out of this no-order. Simultaneously attaining the Way is the true order of our life. Our life is being realized right now; not just our life, everyone's life. Buddha wants us to realize this! When we realize this no-order, then so-called disturbing situations are no longer disturbing; they can then be taken as occasions to encourage our practice, not disturb it.

Someone asked me, "How can I really be responsible for my life?" I asked her, "Do you know who you are?" Not knowing, how can you be responsible for your life? The problem is that what our life actually is and our so-called intellectual understanding of what it is are often two different things. Most of the time we are deceiving ourselves, whether we know it or not. Please be careful about this. Shakyamuni Buddha himself said, "Be a torch for your life." In other words, depend on yourself and be responsible for yourself, not as what you think you are but rather you *as the dharma*. This is very important. You cannot depend on your complaints, on your greed, anger, and ignorance.

So close the gap between Yourself and yourself. Carry this wisdom into your daily life and let your life continue in this way. When you close the gap, that is the best way to take care of your family, of your community, of your life. Then your life becomes delightful, not only for yourself but for the people around you as well.

You do not need to lock yourself in a closet to think about this. With beginner's mind, the mind that sees no separation, you can take care of this gap. This awareness can take place at any moment, under any circumstances. We should also appreciate that our practice is not just for this lifetime only. Shakyamuni Buddha talks about his past lives in the Mahayana sutras. He is not the only one who has had past lives, all of us have had past lives. The more I realize that this practice is not just for this lifetime, the more I appreciate the opportunity to practice together with all of you.

I want you to appreciate your own life, too. Every moment, right now, is nothing other than us, our practice, our life, our realization, our manifestation! Refresh it each moment! Having such a practice not only benefits you and gives you joy, it also inspires others. And vice versa, too. When you live this way, your life will become very different and you will not complain about things. You will become more tolerant and generous. If anything does not go well, you will see this *I* as the responsible person. You will see the other shore as your life this very moment. So regardless of the situation, when you close the gap you can take any situation as the Buddha's life and manage it well.

THE ANSWER IS SIMPLE

DOGEN ZENJI SAID,

When staying at Tendo monastery in China while old master Nyojo was abbot there, we sat zazen until about eleven o'clock at night and got up at about half past two to sit zazen. The abbot sat with the assembly in the *sodo* [the monks' living and practice area] never taking even one night off. While sitting, many monks fell asleep. The abbot walked around hitting them with his fist or his slipper, shaming and encouraging them to wake up. If they continued to sleep, he went to the sodo, rang the bell, and called his attendants to light the candles. On the spur of the moment, he would say such things as: "What is the use of sleeping? Why do you gather in the sodo? Why did you become a monk and enter this monastery? Consider the emperor and officials of the government; who among them leads an easy life?

The emperor governs with justice; the ministers serve with loyalty and down to the commoners. Who leads an easy life without laboring? You have avoided these labors, entered the monastery, but now spend your time wastefully. What on earth for?"

Life and death is the grave matter. Everything is impermanent and changes swiftly. The teaching schools and the Zen schools both emphasize this. This evening or tomorrow morning you may become sick or die. Still you have no idea how your death may come or what kind of sickness you may contract. It is utterly foolish to pass the time meaninglessly sleeping or lying down while you are alive and not practice the Buddha dharma. Since you are like this, the Buddha dharma is dying. When people devotedly practiced zazen, the Buddha dharma flourished throughout the country. As of late, the Buddha dharma is falling into decay because no one promotes zazen.

—*Eihei Dogen*
SHOBOGENZO ZUIMONKI

This passage was written over seven hundred years ago in very different circumstances, and yet it is so vital, so alive! It is a very vivid admonition to us. Although we do not have the lifestyle of a monk or nun living in a monastery, practicing together twenty-four hours a day, basically all of us practice zazen.

Dogen Zenji emphasizes the importance of zazen. Zazen must be done correctly, not loosely, not daydreaming or sleeping, not drowsy zazen. What is the purpose of doing zazen? In order to clarify your aspiration, think on the impermanence of life. We never know when we will die. Reflect upon this seriously: how much do I clarify this grave matter of life and death as a personal fact? What is the best way for me to live?

Dogen Zenji lost his parents when he was a young child, so the urgency of his questioning arose from his own experience of impermanence. Shakyamuni Buddha first became aware of impermanence when he saw people suffering from old age, sickness, and death. When he saw a person who manifested peace in the midst of this world of suffering, he left the comforts of his life to solve this question of the grave matter of life and death. Dogen Zenji says that the power of aspiration is such that when we really want to resolve something, we find a way to do it.

We might feel a little awkward reading the words of master Nyojo or about the quest of Shakyamuni. Having a family, living a secular life, having all kinds of problems—which are the most urgent for us to solve? Do we think about the impermanence of life or how to live more comfortably? We have all kinds of distractions that blind us to this simple matter of impermanence.

Dogen Zenji emphasizes that life and death contain the fact of constant, swift change. In fact, he uses the phrase "Life and death is the grave matter." We chant this verse every evening after zazen:

Life and death are of supreme importance.
Time swiftly passes by and opportunity is lost.
Each of us should strive to awaken.
Awaken. Take heed, do not squander your life.

This is exactly the purpose of doing zazen.

The point is very simple: awakening is Buddha's teaching. This is the key. Awakening is for anybody, everybody! Why do these old masters talk about zazen in such a strict way? Physical strictness does not guarantee awakening. I do not know how many monks were practicing under all these strict masters, but I am one hundred percent sure that not all of them awakened. In fact, awakening has nothing to do with strict or easy practice.

In one of his early writings entitled *Endeavor to Practice the Way* (*Shobogenzo Bendowa*), Dogen Zenji asks eighteen commonly asked questions and answers them himself. The first question is, "Why do you talk so much about the importance of zazen?" His answer is very simple: Because the Buddha did zazen and awakened. What did the Buddha realize? He realized this matter of life and death.

Dogen Zenji says to practice diligently so that you can see the impermanence of your life. The more you feel this impermanence, the more you *have* to know what this life is, what this death is. When we really see this impermanence, we pay much more attention to the principles of attachment and detachment. In a way, detachment is as bad as attachment. And attachment, in a way, is as good as detachment. After all, what is wrong with being attached? Without attachment, we cannot live. If we all are physically detached, if we are detached from our life, then how can we survive?

So where does the trouble come in? This is very simple. The trouble is caused by our self-centered, egocentric ideas. The obstacle to awakening is always *me*, always *I, my, me.* My feeling, my thought, my pain, my idea, all must be eliminated from the beginning because it is a partial or relative view. When we meditate on how we feel or what we think, we remain in a dualistic condition. In the Zen tradition, we avoid this kind of meditation because it is an endless process. When you pursue your thoughts, you can create all kinds of fantastic things. But then what? It doesn't clarify the grave matter of life and death.

What should we do in order to take care of this trouble? Again the answer is simple: Be yourself! Become zazen yourself. Be your true life and death. Be the Buddha! Yet this simple matter is somehow the most difficult to do. How do you awaken to this simple, clear, straightforward fact of who you are? Until you clarify this matter, you will not be at ease. Maybe you can be comfortable for a while, but sooner or later you will come back to this point, for the grave matter will not be settled for you.

Dogen Zenji says, "Life and death is the grave, important matter. There is no life and death, since there is the Buddha in life and death." Consider that life and death itself is no other than peace, no other than nirvana. Nirvana is not some life that will happen one day in the future. It is our life and death right now, right here.

One definition for nirvana is that it is the state of extinction of all sorts of desires that trouble us. In a way, the desire for nirvana itself is attachment. And yet desire is very, very important. For instance, as bodhisattvas we should have the desire to *do* something with our life. Bodhisattvas are those who take boundless vows, and because of these vows, the world gets better. Who is the bodhisattva? A bodhisattva cannot be any person other than yourself. Do you see this? How are you really a bodhisattva?

Each of us has this strong bodhi mind, the mind of awakening. Each of us must awaken. No one can do it for us. Shakyamuni Buddha had to awaken by himself. He struggled for years, and finally he gave up everything and just faced himself. For one week, he did zazen completely. He did not have a teacher, but something supported him, something led him to realization. What was it? Is it supporting you, too? Shakyamuni had a fierce determination. If you really want to awaken, how can *you* do it?

Zazen may be the most direct way. Do it wholeheartedly. Just sitting on the cushion and taking a nap or daydreaming is not zazen. When you sit, don't get involved in any side-business. Be determined to resolve the great matter. Put all your energy into it. When you do this, you will find tremendous strength.

How do you take care of this for yourself? *Where do you miss the point?* This is what you must clarify. I really encourage you. It isn't even a matter or encouraging or discouraging. If you realize this grave matter, that is the very best I can do. This grave matter of life and death is so obvious, so simple, and yet so hard to realize. Even though you are in the midst of the awakened life, you do not realize it.

How do you handle this dilemma?

Your Zazen Is the Zazen of the Buddhas

MY TEACHER YASUTANI ROSHI would say, when you do shikantaza you should have faith. This faith has a particular connotation. This faith is the sense that you can actually do shikantaza. When working on koans, have faith in the fact that you can take care of the koan. Have faith in the fact that your zazen is the zazen of the buddhas and ancestors. You don't need to worry about anything. Just sit and appreciate that your zazen is buddha's zazen. Which buddha? Shakyamuni Buddha is okay.

The buddhas and ancestors are okay. In other words, it is not "you" that is sitting, but buddha.

In Soto Zen there is the expression *honsho myoshu*. *Honsho* means "intrinsic enlightenment," and *myoshu* is "subtle practice." We say that practice and enlightenment are one. How are this practice and your realization one thing? Your zazen is sitting Buddha, or Buddha's zazen, which is realization itself. It is enlightenment itself. It becomes the unsurpassable wisdom (*anuttara samyak sambodhi*) itself. Have this kind of faith.

Our practice often becomes a cause of some kind of effect, like enlightenment. Doing zazen in order to create a certain effect or give rise to certain conditions is the wrong way to do zazen. There are many arguments in the history of Zen on this point. When we say that practice and enlightenment are one, we mean that practice is not a means through which we attain something. Rather, practice is itself a fulfillment of the originally enlightened life. What you are expecting or striving to attain is already here! From the very beginning, the Way is perfectly manifesting right here. Always here, as your life! Realization, or attaining enlightenment, is nothing but becoming aware of this fact.

This direct and clear fact of our life as the intrinsically enlightened life is difficult to see. How can you practice most effectively in order to realize this? It is not a matter of whether you should practice shikantaza or koans but rather how to practice effectively. When you work on koan, is there an awareness of "I am doing koan"? When you sit shikantaza, is there an awareness of "I am doing shikantaza"? If this is so, you need to take care of this *I*. When you work on koan, be koan. When you sit shikantaza, be shikantaza. Let your practice of koan or shikantaza be the zazen of the Buddha. Simply don't let yourself and Buddha be separate. Don't separate yourself from koan or yourself from shikantaza. Don't discriminate between yourself and Buddha, between your life and the intrinsically enlightened life. Sit in this way.

We use many different expressions to convey this. We say it's Buddha or Buddha mind or emptiness or Buddha nature or the supreme Way. All are different expressions for this one life.

I like the koan in which a monk asked Master Gensha, "What is the

Buddha mind?" Gensha answered, "All-beings mind." The monk asks further, "What is all-beings mind?" Gensha says, "Buddha mind." We are like this monk, creating distinctions between this thing and that thing. Of course, discriminating is a very important function of the mind, but we need not create problems with it. When you sit, you often don't know what to do with this discursive mind, which goes on and on and on, endlessly. How do you stop it? You can't stop it! Stopping the mind is not the solution, either. So what do you do?

When you practice, keep in mind that practice and realization are one. Don't make them separate. Allow your zazen to be the manifestation of that fact, and just sit. It's okay if thoughts arise. Just let them go. Try it.

When you practice in this way, then sitting, standing, walking, lying down, all together become zazen. Then a very new vision of life will open up for you. Your zazen is the most precious dharma itself. Let us appreciate the subtle practice of intrinsic enlightenment. Or, let us appreciate the intrinsic realization in our subtle practice. Please do not chase after something else, but appreciate this very life—all the activities of life—as the manifestation of realization.

PRACTICE THE PARAMITAS

THE WEEK OF THE AUTUMN EQUINOX is prajna week in Japan. During this week we contemplate the practice of the six paramitas. These paramitas are *dana,* or giving; *sila,* or precepts; *kshanti,* or patience; *virya*, or effort; *dhyana*, or samadhi; and prajna, or wisdom. When we speak of the ten paramitas, we add *upaya,* or skillful means; *pranidhana,* or vows; *bala,* or power; and the last one, *jnana,* or the wisdom that transcends everything.

In practicing the paramitas, it does not matter whether you are a monk, priest, or layperson. We can equally practice the paramitas. *Param* means "the other shore" and *ita* means "to have reached," so *paramita* means "to have reached the other shore," or nirvana. In other words, the other shore is this shore. The division is eliminated. Wherever we stand, here becomes there, this becomes that. The enlightened life is right here in giving, in effort, and so forth. There is another interesting interpretation for *paramita* that means "the best, the very best," the so-called unsurpassable. So the paramitas are the very best giving, the very best precepts, the very best or unsurpassable effort, the unsurpassable samadhi, the unsurpassable wisdom.

Dana, the first paramita, is the unsurpassable giving, the very best giving. What is unsurpassable giving? Quite often when we give something, we naturally expect some kind of return. We are not giving unconditionally. There are many aspects to consider regarding giving. On the one hand, we consider the three wheels of giving: the giver, the receiver, and that which is given. We ask how, when, and where giving can best occur. We can appreciate this endlessly, like space expanding in the ten directions. On the other hand, it could all be pinned down to a single point.

We have a saying, "The giver, the recipient, and the things given are none other than emptiness and tranquility." This is the meaning of dana paramita. The fundamental teaching of the Buddha is no-self. Buddha is selfless—the giver is selfless, the recipient is selfless, and the things given are selfless. Regarding giving, Dogen Zenji said, "Only fools think that other people benefit at their expense. It is not so. Both benefit." This is so because life is altogether as one. But we are so nearsighted that we see only a very small part of the one life. The more self-centered and selfish we are, the less we see.

There is a story of a young boy named Sessan, who was said to be a previous incarnation of Shakyamuni Buddha. Even as a young boy, Sessan was hungry for the truth of life, so he went to the mountains to find a teacher. One day while deep in the mountains, Sessan heard a voice saying, "Everything is impermanent. This is the dharma of being born and dying." Hearing this, Sessan was deeply moved. "Where does this voice come from?" he wondered. He looked around, but saw no one. Then he heard the voice again, "Everything is impermanent. This is the dharma of being born and dying." Then Sessan saw a fierce-looking demon. But Sessan was so eager to learn the truth of life, he felt no fear. Approaching the demon, the young boy asked, "There must be another part to this poem. Please let me know the rest of it."

The demon replied, "No, I can't. I'm so hungry I can't say another word." Sessan pleaded, "Please! I ask this favor. What do you eat? I'll get it for you." The demon answered, "I eat fresh human flesh." Sessan said, "If you teach me the rest of this poem, I'll offer my body to you." The demon recited the poem: "Realize the state of no-life, no-death, no-change. See the emptiness. Then you will be in nirvana, comfortable and peaceful." Upon hearing this, Sessan cut his finger and, with his blood wrote the poem on the trees and rocks. Then he jumped into the demon's mouth and, at that instant, the demon transformed into the god Indra.

This story brings out another interesting aspect of giving. Dana is not limited to giving something to someone. It's giving yourself away! The Japanese word is *kisha*, "willing to abandon" or "cast away." That's giving.

Our standard for unsurpassable giving is: the three wheels are empty. In other words, when the giver, receiver, and things given are empty and peaceful, there is unconditional giving. When the giver, receiver, and things given are empty, then we don't have any ideas attached to them; in fact, we don't know who is the giver, who is the receiver, and what are the things given. Unconditional means that all these things are in their so-called empty nature, there is no gain and no loss, energy just flows in a natural way. Giving is at its unsurpassable best when done in this way.

In our practice, what to give is divided into categories such as material possessions. This reminds me of the story of the enlightened Layman Pang. He was a rich man who dumped all of his possessions into the ocean. Seeing him do this, his friends became upset and demanded, "Why don't you give these things to others who can use them?" Layman Pang answered, "These things are not good for me. How can I give them to others?" Sometimes, having possessions can hurt us. Of course, when we know how to use things without any particular attachment or detachment, it doesn't matter whether we have possessions or not. So being selfless, we can abandon things according to necessity or the situation, and it benefits others.

Another category is giving the dharma. For example, giving a dharma talk is sharing the dharma. In a dharma talk, the giver is turning the dharma wheel, the receiver is also turning the dharma wheel, and the dharma itself is turning. All together, all are turning in emptiness, in perfect intimacy, which is the most free, most precious way that the dharma turns. We are helping others to realize the most important thing in life, which is accomplishing the Way. The *Lotus Sutra* says, "Why do buddhas appear in the world? To lead everyone to buddhas' wisdom." My teacher Koryu Roshi's dharma grandfather used this as a koan. Buddha himself spent forty years of his life leading people like ourselves to realization. When the dharma is given, the giver is receiving the listeners' response. The listeners are receiving and they are also giving. In a sense, we can say that everything is giving and receiving, isn't it true?

Dana paramita is perhaps considered the most characteristic of Mahayana practices because it most obviously involves others. But this applies to all the other paramitas as well. In fact, each paramita contains all the others. For instance, in prajna or wisdom paramita, we practice selflessness, the empty condition of life. When we practice this wisdom, compassion arises naturally. This compassion is nothing but dana, giving. Being selfless, we can't help but give. When we practice selflessly, we are functioning freely as all the paramitas.

We emphasize the importance of bodhisattva practice. In other words, sharing with others is emphasized over one's own accomplishment. How can we truly share and appreciate this Buddha dharma? Although the three wheels are unconditioned and empty and we know this unsurpassable dharma can be freely given and received, yet somehow the wheel is stuck. It does not turn smoothly. Where do we get stuck? We can check ourselves against the three aspects of ignorance, anger, and greed. When our wheel is not turning quite smoothly, what are we ignoring? How can we help each other so that our wheels turn smoothly?

Of course, the wheel not turning smoothly is itself no other than the functioning of the dharma. We are the giver and we are the receiver and we are what is given, we are the dharma ourselves. Nevertheless, *how* is this wheel to be turned? Don't forget, this give-and-take is always mutual, for no one is fully awakened unless the whole world is awakened. So my position and your position are the same.

Who is the giver? Who is the receiver? What is being given and received? We are giving and receiving these paramitas. We are giving and receiving giving, discipline, effort, patience, samadhi, wisdom. These are not mere principles. *How* are we giving and receiving all of these paramitas? Each of us is equally involved, each of us is completely responsible. We all are the Buddha dharma. Regarding this, Dogen Zenji says that the ocean does not decline any water, but rather it accepts any kind of water. That is why it exists as the ocean. And that oceanlike life is the life of each of us, do you see? How much are we truly appreciating, digesting, and turning our life in this way?

As a standard of giving, we say that the best thing to give is no-fear. How do we do this? In the *Heart Sutra,* Avalokiteshvara Bodhisattva does the practice of prajna paramita and relieves misfortune and pain. Prajna paramita is anything, everything! Literally everything! Avalokiteshvara Bodhisattva, in relieving all our fears and troubles, gives no-fear. How is this done? When we don't have our self-centered ideas, then there is no-fear. So who is truly Avalokiteshvara Bodhisattva? You know the answer, don't you?

Each of us has abundant dharma to share. So in doing this paramita practice, the practice of reaching the other shore, all of us know that the other shore is right beneath our feet. Right here! Always here! Wherever you go, that is where here is! How can we make our realization clear and appreciate these wonderful paramitas as the life of each of us?

ON CEREMONIAL ACTION

IT IS INTERESTING TO REFLECT on how the most basic routines of our lives are conducted in an orderly way within a particular form. When our actions are conducted in this way, they become ceremony. What is ceremony?

The original implications of ceremony in Judeo-Christian culture reveal how we live and point to what is missing in our life now. In Latin, "ceremony" is *caerimonia,* which is related to *cura,* meaning "cure," the act of healing or of being healed. In other words, ceremony is an act that cures or heals, or by which something is healed. In having a ceremony or in doing ceremonial action, we must ask, what is healed? By what?

The word *heal* means to be healthy, to be whole and sound. To make our life healthy is ceremonial. In order to live a healthy life, we live ceremonially every day regardless of our culture, country, or race. From morning to night, we live our lives through rituals, don't we? We get up in the morning, wash our face, brush our teeth, and eat, going about these simple routines in an orderly way. When eating, we have the ritual of using a fork, knife, and plate. At work we act ceremonially when we greet our colleagues in a particular way.

From time to time, many of you express your discomfort with ritual. Most of us prefer informality or casualness. But regardless of whether something is formal or informal, still there is form. The definition of ceremony also includes the word *law,* the laws of life. From morning until night, our life is continuous ritual, governed by rules, regulations, and laws. Behaving informally, can we follow the laws or regulations that are essential to living a healthy life?

We can say that living an informal life is more comfortable for us. But in fact, something is ignored when we do even simple things without an understanding of ceremony. What are we ignoring? How do we take care of ourselves in each moment? When the time comes to get up in the morning, just get up. It is a seemingly simple thing, but how do you do it? By doing it in an orderly way, you regulate yourself and your life. When you do these actions casually, you miss something.

Is being informal really more comfortable? Some of you wear formal sitting clothes in the zendo and some dress rather informally. Certain informal clothing is permissible. I do not mind if you wear long pants and a long-sleeved shirt rather than a robe. But, for example, during the summer when it is hot, if you come to sit wearing short pants, you may think you will be comfortable, but this might not necessarily be the case. And vice versa; being overdressed would also be funny.

So following a particular form can cure us of our tendency to become too casual or disorderly and therefore unhealthy. In the zendo we should have a sense of being together. When you do certain things in your own way simply because you want to, this causes disharmony. Situations are regulated in a particular way. Ceremony means to follow that way! This is the best way to be healthy.

From time to time I have been emphasizing the importance of individual action. But I think that individual action and group action are the same. So ideally, ceremonial action should have the individual as the center of a group, of a sangha, of a country, of society or world. By taking care of things in a ceremonial way, we become unified. We come together as one, staying away from our own self-centered interests, do you see?

Who do you think creates the casual, disorderly way of life? *I* do. Our ego does. Ceremony can be understood as a form or discipline by which we avoid self-centeredness, which causes our difficulties. Self-centered living creates trouble not only for others but also for oneself. Usually we do not understand ceremony in this way, but the definition I am presenting here is actually based on your own Judeo-Christian tradition. In the wisdom of your own tradition and culture, you have inherited ceremony as a way to regulate your life.

Regarding healing, there are some interesting points to consider. For instance, sickness can be a symptom of disorderliness of the mind, emotion, psyche, body, whatever. In one way or another, we are all sick until we have become unified and live a balanced life. Of course, we can be physically ill and still live ceremonially, in some balance.

How do we keep ourselves in order? By examining our body and mind. We are ceremonial by balancing ourselves and externals. In order to harmonize yourself, regulate your life from morning to night. When we live in this so-called formal way, sickness or the unsound life is avoided. And when we do not, we create a troubled life.

We practice this Buddha Way, which is literally the laws or teachings of the Buddha. Dogen Zenji says, "To practice the Buddha Way is to study oneself. To study oneself is to forget the self." What happens when you forget the self? The Buddha Way is revealed as your own life. This is the purpose of ceremony. Dogen Zenji further says, "To forget the self is to be confirmed or to be enlightened by the ten thousand dharmas." To forget the self is to be enlightened by everything, the order and forms that we live by from morning to night. This is the enlightened life itself.

Bowing is an important act in the Buddhist tradition. In Zen the most respectful bow is the bow in which our knees, elbows, and head all touch the ground. In Tibet and India, some bows are done by literally lying flat on the ground. This signifies the complete absence of one's own ego or self—just complete obeisance to the laws that are the order of life. Bowing with absence of ego is the most polite bow. How can you unify yourself with Yourself as well as with anything, everything? This is bowing. This is the ceremonial action of forgetting the self and being enlightened by bowing.

The same thing could be said for brushing our teeth and washing our face. In Dogen Zenji's *Shobogenzo Senmen*, he writes about how to wash the face. Washing the face is nothing but the treasury of the true dharma eye itself. Washing the face is the unsurpassable Way. Dogen Zenji even writes about using the toilet and how to wipe your bottom. He explains all this in detail. It is somewhat extreme ceremonial action!

When we read about this kind of detailed ceremonial action, it seems almost ridiculous, but Dogen Zenji is serious. This is nothing but enlightened action. It is life itself. By being ceremonial, we can order ourselves. If we have even the slightest idea of like or dislike, of what *I* want, we simply cannot be ceremonial in this way. In other words, such ceremonial actions in themselves become a powerful medicine. Unfortunately, it is so powerful that not many people can follow it.

We practice zazen. When we truly do zazen, everything is taken care of. This is ceremony. When we carefully understand our life, every bit of our life becomes ceremonial action, very orderly, formal action. This action is not for the sake of formality but for a healthy, sound life. When we live this way, healing or being healed is unnecessary. The enlightened life is an orderly, ordinary life. We should take care to live this way. This is ceremony, do you see?

PART TWO

Clarify the Great Matter

What Is Koan?

What is the point of our practice? We are not just sitting on a cushion. Someone said to me this morning, "Roshi, one person sitting could not bear the pain and he left. I feel sorry about that." I feel sorry for this person, too. Definitely our practice cannot be just bearing pain and being discouraged. Dogen Zenji said zazen has to be comfortable. He says, "Zazen is the dharma gate of bliss and joy." Zazen should not be torture. Please try to sit comfortably. It is okay to use a chair or a bench. It is a shame, almost a crime, to let people get so discouraged that they feel they must give up.

So this leads us back to the point: What is practice? What is zazen for?

We are so goal oriented. Of course, there is nothing wrong with having a goal. But if there is any goal in practice, what is it? I am sure you have set up some kind of goal for yourself. Is it clear why you are practicing and what you are doing? We each know to some degree or other that our discriminating or discursive mind gives us problems. There is nothing wrong with this mind in and of itself. Without discrimination, life would be chaos. And yet because of this discriminating mind, we create problems for ourselves and others. How we solve this problem is the koan.

We use expressions such as koan practice or working on koans. What does this mean? When we embody a koan that we're working on, then that koan is in realization. Otherwise, even though we talk about koan practice, it does not mean much. So we have to clarify this very fundamental point in order to make our practice truly meaningful and worthwhile.

There is a famous koan of the Sixth Patriarch Hui-neng, who established the Southern Ch'an School in seventh-century China, and his disciple Nangaku Ejo. Hui-neng asked Ejo, "What comes thus?" Since this was a conversation, the Sixth Patriarch may have used the word *thus* very colloquially. It is a very common expression, like "Where do you come from?" or "What comes like this?" Perhaps Hui-neng simply asked Ejo, "Who are you?" Ejo answered, "When anything is said about it, you miss the mark." In other words, even when one word of expression is attached to it, then it is not it. What does this mean?

In order to answer, Ejo had spent eight years penetrating the Sixth Patriarch's question. What was he doing during these eight years? He was trying to come up with something, and each time he tried, he failed. What made him fail? Somehow trying itself made him fail. It did not matter how fine a definition he gave to *Who am I?*. Finally Ejo gave up. When he gave up, he realized the answer. Or it could have happened vice versa, he may have seen that all this effort to find out *Who am I?* was unnecessary, and then he realized it! That is the realization of koan; this is seeing our original face as the unity of absolute and relative. This koan has always been realizing itself since the beginningless beginning. It is fact!

What does "comes thus" mean? Be thus! As this! What else is there to say about it? Are you seeing this very being itself and then objectifying it? You have got to be one with it! That is what Dogen Zenji means when he says that practice and realization are one. If we set up any goal as such, then there is a split. There is something extra which hinders us from seeing what our life actually is.

This reminds me of Tenkei Denson Zenji's phrase on Avalokiteshvara

Bodhisattva. The *Heart Sutra* begins thus: "Avalokiteshvara Bodhisattva doing deep prajna paramita." Tenkei Zenji says that Avalokiteshvara Bodhisattva is *your* name. Isn't it wonderful? I really love Tenkei Zenji's expression; it is a very, very simple and clear-cut statement. And when you really take Avalokiteshvara as your name, when there is no separation between yourself and Avalokiteshvara, right there the koan is in realization. Avalokiteshvara is doing deep prajna paramita. That deep prajna paramita is also Nangaku Ejo's answer. "When anything is said about it, it is off." When there is even a tiny, tiny bit of discrepancy between who I am and *who I am,* between Avalokiteshvara and myself, it is off.

You *are* Avalokiteshvara Bodhisattva. That is the koan. How to practice that koan? How to make that realization your practice? When you do this, your life is marvelous. Marvelous in the sense that Avalokiteshvara Bodhisattva realizes the state of no-fear and gives no-fear to everybody.

I believe that giving no-fear is the very best thing we can do. Giving no-fear is true compassion. Being compassionate, *what do we give? What do we take away?* We take away pain, suffering. Do you want to take it away? Then give no-fear. All of us are Avalokiteshvara Bodhisattva. How do we take it as our practice, as our life, to manifest no-fear? When we do, we are truly practicing koan.

KOAN AND SHIKANTAZA

IN JAPAN WE HOLD a special sesshin,* during which we express our gratitude toward the three benevolences. Generally these benevolences are the Three Treasures of Buddha, Dharma, and Sangha; our teachers, parents, nation, and all sentient beings; and all beings in the six worlds.†️ We understand sentient beings as living human beings and also, in a

---

*An intensive Zen retreat—Eds.

† The "six worlds" refer to the six realms of existence: hell, hungry ghost, animal, human, titan, and god.—Eds.

broader sense, as everything. We should be grateful for everything, literally everything.

Showing our gratitude for just the Three Treasures is sufficient because these treasures are all-inclusive. Everything is included in the Buddha Treasure, in the Dharma Treasure, in the Sangha Treasure. At their most condensed point, what are these treasures? They are the life of each of us. We express our gratitude toward ourselves as well as toward everything, not as two separate things but both as one life. Do you see? Whether you realize it or not, this one life is the most fundamental koan. What does that mean? It means that at every moment, our life is the unity of the absolute and the relative, of oneness and diversity. This very concrete and profound aspect of each of our lives is koan, absolute reality, fact.

Shikantaza and koan are seemingly two different practices. They are different and yet they are the same. This sameness and difference are our practice, and we appreciate the Buddha dharma in this way. In what sense are shikantaza and koan the same? What is shikantaza? What is koan? And most important, *how* do we practice shikantaza, *how* do we practice koan? How much are you getting out of it? Of course, on one hand, there is nothing to get. On the other hand, there is immeasurable value in these practices.

We can say that shikantaza is doing zazen as the manifestation of your life as the Buddha Way, as the Buddha dharma itself. When you truly do zazen in this way, your life functions as the triple gem—as the Buddha, Dharma, and Sangha—as the unity of these Three Treasures. You do not look for anything else because everything is here with you. Who is you? It is not what you think you are, but you *as* the Three Treasures. How you do shikantaza is very important. If you do not sit as the Buddha Way, you are not doing shikantaza.

What is koan practice? Koan practice is to embody this life as the koan. What is koan? *Ko* means "public," such as a governmental or authoritative position. One definition of *ko* is a document issued by the government that has authoritative value. The Chinese character *ko* has two parts. The top part, which looks like the figure 8 in two strokes with space in between, has the implication of being separate, or apart from the other. The bottom part means *I, myself.* In other words, when there is separation, the *I* is there.

Ko is a universal, or absolute, position as opposed to *shi* or *shian,* which is the position based on our own ideas. *Shi* means "I, me, my ideas, my understanding." *Shian* is something private, personal. The more we base our life on shian, the more problems we have. If we base our life on *ko,* then we are just as we are, without our personal thoughts. Isn't it interesting? When we really come to the point, a koan is very ordinary. *Just as we are* is the koan, it cannot be shian, based on our personal ideas. How can we ourselves be as koan?

In the Soto tradition, another definition of *ko* is "equal and unequal existing together." It is not that some things are right and other things are wrong, but rather that evenness and unevenness, equal and not equal, are all together *ko.* Even regarding ourselves—male and female, young and old, tall and short, heavy and light, having a beard and not having a beard, having hair and not having hair—we are different and yet one, the same. This is also *ko.*

According to Senne, who studied with Dogen Zenji, *an* means "to maintain one's own intrinsic position." Each of us as we are, as male or female, tall or short, however we are, has our own relative position. That relative position and its intrinsic nature are not separate. In other words, regardless of the differences in appearance or conditioning, we are in a way the same. This is true not only for human beings, but literally for anything, everything.

We are all of equal intrinsic value. This is the value of no-value, in the sense of emptiness. We are conditioned as male or female, tall or short, or however we are. That is called the Dharma Treasure. Yet we are also the Buddha Treasure, which is not at all conditioned. The unity of the Dharma Treasure and the Buddha Treasure is the Sangha Treasure, and that is true for each of us. That means that each of us, as different as we are, as conditioned as we are, is the Buddha Treasure. We are the Buddha Treasure! As we are, we are the Dharma Treasure! We have our intrinsic nature and our relative position. That is the koan. Dogen Zenji talks about this manifestation as the *genjo* koan, the embodiment of koan *as your life.* How do you appreciate this manifestation of koan as your life?

The *Record of the Transmission of the Lamp* numbers seventeen hundred Zen masters, each with his own koans. So koans are literally numberless. Anything could be a koan. How to really appreciate it? We can look at koan practice as a kind of scheme or expediency, where we expect a result. But the point is not the number of koans you solve or practicing koans as something apart from yourself. If you are not realizing your life as the manifestation of koan, then you are reinforcing another kind of ego, which is not good. The important point is how do you realize the absolute and the relative in your life?

The same can be said of shikantaza. I know there are people who believe that shikantaza is superior to koan practice. They even speak badly about the practice of koan Zen. The point is how are we practicing shikantaza? How much are we manifesting or realizing the real value, the richness and boundless merit contained in the practice of shikantaza? Dogen Zenji calls this self-fulfilled samadhi. Self-fulfilled samadhi literally contains everything, not restricted to my way or our way of practice, not better than something or someone else. It is not something that human beings create, rather it is the subtle dharma that is handed down without discrepancy from ancestor to ancestor to now.

This self-fulfilled samadhi is the key to checking whether your practice is right zazen, whether you appreciate yourself as the treasure transmitted from buddha to buddha, from ancestor to ancestor. Self-fulfilled samadhi is all-inclusiveness. Each of us is equally living this all-inclusive life. And when you really do zazen in this way, it naturally becomes shikantaza. When you work on koan, the koan naturally becomes your life. Furthermore, your life all together becomes nothing but the *genjo* koan, the manifestation of *that*.

Please do not forget that your life itself is the practice. Practice is no other than your life. Live each moment as the manifestation of koan regardless of how it goes one moment after another, not judging according to your ideas. In the very beginning of the *Genjo Koan,* Dogen Zenji says, "All dharmas are Buddha dharma." Everything exists. And "All dharmas are without self." Nothing exists. Dogen Zenji continues,

"Buddha dharma goes beyond, with, and without self." Once again, everything exists.

What does "without self" mean? This is very important. "Without self" is expounded in the *Heart Sutra* as emptiness. What is emptiness? This body and mind. This body and mind is empty. If you do not see this emptiness, you are seeing something else. In another part of the *Genjo Koan*, Dogen Zenji says, "To study the Buddha Way is to study oneself. To study oneself is to forget the self." Be without self. What happens when you are without self? Dogen Zenji says, "To forget the self is to be enlightened by the ten thousand dharmas." When you are without self, you are enlightened, confirmed by literally anything, everything.

Dogen Zenji continues, "To be confirmed by ten thousand dharmas is to free one's own body and mind as well as that of others." In this passage we also realize Shakyamuni Buddha's remarks upon his enlightenment. Upon seeing the morning star, Shakyamuni said, "I and the great earth, all beings, simultaneously attain the Way." In other words, the liberation is not just of oneself, but of anything, everything, everybody. All are liberated. And Dogen Zenji concludes that paragraph, "That traceless enlightenment continues forever." Allow that traceless enlightenment to manifest *as is*. This is your life at this very moment, now.

When I was studying with Yasutani Roshi, he emphasized over and over the importance of checking our practice from the intrinsic and the experiential perspectives. The principles that Dogen Zenji talks about are the intrinsic perspective: what is the Buddha dharma? The experiential side is *you*. *You* must experience the Buddha dharma by yourself. Otherwise, you cannot appreciate it as the treasure. Of course, regardless of whether you experientially appreciate the dharma or not, it is what it is. That is the intrinsic side of it. Regardless of what you think, even your crazy thinking itself is nothing but *that,* do you see? It is no other than the dharma. The dharma manifests as your crazy thinking; it manifests in every way under every circumstance. But in order to truly appreciate it, we must experience it. Dogen Zenji says that traceless realization is already manifesting as your life in each moment. Let it be so.

This practice is truly wonderful. Our Buddha ancestors have shown us how to appreciate our life in this way. We should be most grateful for their benevolences. However much we do will never be too much. The best way to repay our debt to our buddha ancestors is to do true shikantaza and manifest our life as the realization of koan, or manifest koan as the realization of our life. Whatever your practice, the important point is this life that you are living and how to take care of it. Under certain conditions and involvements, a good thing is good, a poor thing is poor, an inadequate thing is inadequate. When you truly appreciate that all the dharmas are Buddha dharma and all dharmas are without self, your life will unfold naturally and you will know what to do.

RAISE THE BODHI MIND

IN HIS *PRECAUTIONS ON PRACTICING THE WAY* (*Gakudo Yojin-shu*), Dogen Zenji emphasizes the importance of raising the bodhi mind. Dogen Zenji expresses it beautifully: We raise the bodhi mind not just one time but a hundred times, a thousand times, ten thousand times. Raise that bodhi mind!

All of you are raising the bodhi mind. What *is* bodhi mind? It literally means enlightened mind, awakened mind. The very first time that you decide to seek the very best way to live is beginner's mind, very fresh, first mind. Brand-new mind! And each time that you seek the very best way to live, you raise the bodhi mind. When you raise the bodhi mind, at that time you are awakening yourself. When you raise that mind the first time, at that very moment the Way is perceived. The mind with which you seek enlightenment is also the bodhi mind, the mind of enlightenment.

Seeing the impermanence of life is also raising the bodhi mind. What is this impermanence? Everything is constantly changing. If we say that anything is permanent, it is not quite right. But is this true? I believe in something that is permanent. I truly believe that the life of this *it*—this

Buddha nature—is permanent in the sense that it is always here with me, as my life!

Shakyamuni Buddha expounds this in the *Lotus Sutra:*

> Even though as an expediency I enter into nirvana, my life is not going to be extinguished. Constantly, I am residing here [at Mount Gridhrakuta]* and unceasingly expound the dharma.

What is constantly residing here? What is the life of coming and going and yet never leaving? How is Mount Gridhrakuta realized in your life right now? Wherever you are is the place where Buddha expounds the dharma. So raise the bodhi mind, that mind of the enlightened heart, and see this impermanence of life that is constantly residing here!

In his *Precautions on Practicing the Way*, Dogen Zenji emphasizes the importance of faith. He says that when you practice the Buddha Way, you must have faith in the fact that you are already in the midst of the Way! There is no confusion, no wavering; it is very straightforward. Keep away from all upside-down views. In our life and the life of the buddhas and ancestors, is there any part that must be increased or decreased, added or subtracted? No such change is necessary. There is no mistake or error. Your life in the midst of the Way means that your life is the Way itself! Have faith in this! *This* life is the life of all the buddhas and ancestors. They have all experienced their lives in this way.

Dogen Zenji is so kind. He does not tell us just to blindly believe in the Buddha Way. First, he says, raise strong faith in the fact that your life is one with the Buddha Way. Then, clarify this! Experience the Way as your life and experience your life as the Way. Transmute that faith into wisdom and according to that wisdom, practice! You do not need to worry about when you are going to be enlightened as the result of your practice. Trust yourself! You are no other than the Buddha Way itself to begin with!

In Zen practice we speak of three prerequisites for practice: great

---

* The location where the Buddha preached the *Lotus Sutra* (referred to earlier as Vulture Peak)—Eds.

faith, great doubt, and great determination. In a way, these are contradictory. If you have great faith, where does great doubt come from? When you really have great faith, that is enough. But a person who has such great faith is hard to find, for it must be faith that you and the Buddha Way are one, not faith in something that comes out of your own thoughts. This is an important distinction, do you see?

Great questioning, or great doubt, is to investigate this very point. You say, "The Buddha says such and such; Dogen Zenji says such and such; I believe in such and such. And yet, somehow I can't really accept how my life is. Where do I get stuck? Why can't I have such majestic faith that takes care of everything?" The more you seriously penetrate into faith, such questions will simultaneously occur.

So you question, what is this? What is great faith? What is the Buddha Way? What is the dharma? Who am I? What is it? The more serious faith you have, the more serious the questioning that may or may not arise. If this questioning does arise, it is ideal to focus on. Then the third prerequisite, great determination, naturally follows. The more serious you are in resolving this matter, the more desperate you feel, the stronger your determination becomes, and a clearer, quicker answer is realized. What is that answer? The answer is already there as your life. Your life is no other than that!

By such an awakening, you assure yourself that this life has always been the Way. The awakening experience is important, but relatively speaking, it is rather minor. What is more important? This life that we are constantly living minute after minute is most important. Our practice is here! Now! How to do it? In fact, you *are* doing it. Please, I do not know how to say it: focus or unfocus. Focus in the sense that this life is the life of the buddhas! Live it and clarify it! On the other hand, if we are trying to figure out what to do with our so-called limited or confined conscious mind, then unfocus. Let go of that. Forget about it!

Have good trust in yourself. Have good faith in your practice. Sit well and unconditionally open yourself up. Experience your zazen as the zazen of the buddhas and the awakened ones. This is the most effective, most appropriate life to share together.

REALIZE YOUR LIFE AS KOAN

WE HAVE A COMMON SAYING in the monastery that in order to understand the master's talks on koans, we must spend three years practicing. In other words, it is not so easy to understand what the master is presenting. How much you appreciate the ancient cases is up to you. The *Blue Cliff Record,* one of the major Zen koan collections, contains many different prefaces, appreciatory verses, commentaries, and short critical remarks called capping phrases by different masters. Each of these comments is a gem. Those who appreciate it, appreciate it almost endlessly, just one comment, just one case. But koans are not limited to these ancient cases. You can create koans, too. I want to share with you what koans are as the realization of your life.

As I mentioned before, *ko* in koan is often understood as a government document that has certain authoritative value. But another definition of *ko* is to "make unevenness even." This is a very interesting definition. And *an* means "let it be," whatever it is. Could be you, could be me, could be anything. Let a person be as he or she is. In other words, just let it be *as is.*

How can we make the unevenness even? In our life, everything is unique in that no two things are exactly the same. Everything is different, or uneven—amazingly so. For each of us, our gender is different, our length of life is different, the way we study is different, our jobs are different. Even how much we eat is different. What does it mean to make this unevenness, all these differences, even? How is it possible?

It *is* possible. Being different, each is totally absolute! Each difference is totally complete in itself. And being absolute and complete, it is equal to other differences that are absolute and complete. So *ko* means being different and yet equal. We can say that the absolute makes the unevenness even. We can call it emptiness, or we can call it true self, our original face, *Mu.* Whatever name we use, it is the *unshakeable* aspect. So regardless of how much you complain about the unevenness of your life, there is an unshakable aspect to it!

To really see this absolute aspect is the major point of koan. When you truly see it, you see the relative side without much problem. Everybody, everything, is *just as is* in a particular position. Having a certain status, a certain form, one manifests as that absolute aspect. That is nothing but realization itself, isn't it? We talk as though Ultimate Reality and ordinary reality are two different things. No! Form is emptiness. This body, legs, and hands are empty. All our mental functions such as feelings, sensations, thoughts, are also empty, and therefore, identical.

The absolute values of your life and of everything else are identical. When you truly see this very important point, right there the koan is solved. So without practicing any ancient koans, you can be enlightened and live your life in perfect realization. This is the kind of koan practice I want to share with you. How can we work with this effectively in our practice?

There are many traps relating to our practice. One very tricky trap is this idea of emptiness, of your true self. For instance, Dogen Zenji talks about different kinds of diligent effort. One effort is to do good. But what is meant by that? How do you define it? Dogen Zenji defines doing good as *to realize your true self*. What is that true self? Where is it? We think that there is something that is called true self that exists beyond good or bad, right or wrong, this or that. That is a big trap. Are you looking for something that exists somewhere else, not in your life as is? That is the biggest trap.

In fact, we are already caught in the trap. Why? Because we are human. That means we are conditioned. So be aware that you are already trapped. At the same time, there really is no trap. Why? Because our conditioned self is our true self. Our life *as it is* is in perfect realization. This is a very sneaky aspect. We think something like a trap exists, waiting for us to fall in. But remarkably, there is no such trap to begin with. To think that there is a trap is itself the worst trap, for what trap can there be when our life *as it is,* with all its aspects, including so-called pitfalls and traps, is the enlightened Way? This is what is meant by making the unevenness even. If we can see this in a direct way, then we are realizing our life as koan.

Koans are also symbolic of our life. Take the koan of Master Isan's Buffalo. Master Isan told a monk, "A hundred years later, I'll be born in front of the temple as a buffalo. Beside the buffalo, the name Monk Isan is written. If you call it a buffalo, it's Monk Isan. And if you call it Monk Isan, it's a buffalo. How do you call it?"

This koan has a further checking point. Daito Kokushi, the second Japanese patriarch in the Rinzai lineage, is considered to be the reincarnation of Master Unmon. Master Unmon lived in China about three hundred to four hundred years prior to him. If Master Daito is the incarnation of Master Unmon, where has he been these three hundred years? That is the koan. What does it have to do with you? That is the point: *What does this have to do with you?* What kind of relationship does it have with your own life?

How can you embody this koan? It could be written on your forehead. Where is the name Shakyamuni Buddha? When you call it Shakyamuni Buddha, it is you! And when it is called you, it is Shakyamuni Buddha. *How do you call it?* Right now, this moment! Do not wait a hundred years to be born somewhere else. *How do you call it?*

We say that every moment we are being born and we are dying. How are we being born and dying moment to moment? This is a wonderful koan. When you know this, you will have no problem enjoying yourself as the incarnation of Shakyamuni Buddha himself. Or of Bodhidharma, or Monk Isan, or a buffalo, or whoever you wish.

Koan is the manifestation of ultimate reality. What is ultimate reality? It is your very life! How is your very life manifesting right now? Is it manifesting as the realization of koan? When you truly manifest koan, then your treasure house will open by itself and you will use it as you wish. Use koan as the key to open the treasure house. Once you open it, what is inside is also koan. And the one who is turning the key is also koan. That treasure is also nothing but yourself, your life. When you realize this, then the koan is in manifestation.

Pain, Fear, and Frustration

SOMETIMES OUR LIFE SEEMS to go to all kinds of so-called negative extremes. When this happens, how do we take care of our frustrations, anxiety, pain, sorrows, even despair? The point is how do we put balance in our life? What kind of standards do we use?

In the Four Noble Truths, Shakyamuni Buddha speaks the truth of suffering. We know that happiness never continues forever. Ironically, the more happiness we have, the more pain we have when we lose this happiness. Generally speaking, birth and death are understood as the main causes of suffering. Birth, sickness, old age, and death are all suffering. To be born is to live and become sick, to become old. Dogen Zenji tells us that there is a buddha within sickness; there is a buddha in the midst of getting old; there is a buddha within suffering. More precisely, being born is the life of buddha, being sick is the life of buddha, getting old is the life of buddha, death is nothing but the life of buddha. It is the same life as our life. Do not discriminate between the life of buddha and your life.

One of our members recently learned that her mother has terminal cancer. Her mother has not been told of this, so the daughter wrote and asked me, "Shall I tell her or not?" I wrote back a passage from Dogen Zenji, "Birth and death is the life of the Buddha." I don't know what she told her mother, since her mother is not Buddhist. Is it difficult for you to take death as the life of buddha?

Dogen Zenji also said, "When the Buddha is within birth and death, there is neither birth nor death." This is a wonderful koan. If there is no birth, no death, then what exists? Answer me. What exists? Just buddha. We are being born and dying simultaneously. Each moment we are being born and each moment, dying. Instant birth and death. This means that in every moment our life is brand new. We are living this fresh, new life all the time, and yet we experience so many fears and frustrations.

Of the Four Noble Truths, the fourth, the Eightfold Path, is the most important, for it talks about how we can take care of suffering. In the Eightfold Path, the Buddha begins with right understanding, or right view. This sense of right is not limited to a conventional sense of right and wrong, but means a total or complete understanding. We should understand life and the aspects of life in a proper way. Right understanding is followed by right thought, speech, conduct, livelihood, effort, mindfulness, and concentration, or samadhi. Samadhi leads us back to right understanding. What is right samadhi? This kind of samadhi is one of the very crucial bases for making decisions. When we have it, we transcend this restricted *I*. If we do not transcend this *I,* we create delusions and we suffer pain, fear, and frustrations.

The Eightfold Path begins with right understanding, which takes care of ninety percent of the pain in life. What makes it right? What is right and what is wrong? In one way or another, all of us have some kind of standard by which we make value judgments, by which we judge whether something is good or bad, right or wrong, adequate or inadequate.

In this regard, there are four aspects to consider when we have decisions to make or actions to take. The aspects are time, place, the people involved, and amount. These could be applied to any situation with our commonsense understanding. For instance, we must take into account the people involved in the situation before we can take action or make certain decisions. We also consider the circumstances, the place, and how much we can do. If we pay attention to these four aspects, we can judge fairly well what to do.

In the *Nirvana Sutra,* we find the Buddha's last sermon on the Eight Awarenesses of the Enlightened Person. It is somewhat similar to the Eightfold Path of his first sermon. I want to emphasize the first two awarenesses: wanting little and knowing how to be satisfied. The first awareness is having few or fewer desires. It does not say not to want anything, but rather to have fewer desires. There is wonderful wisdom here. Want little of the things that we do not have. With just this awareness, our life can be fairly well sustained.

How much should we want? How do we know if it is too little or too much? And what kind of things should we want? In a way, wanting little is a very clear guideline, but it is not easy to achieve. What would be good guidelines for practicing wanting little? You already have everything you need! So it is not a matter of setting up artificial guidelines. Look deeply into yourself. I think you know the answer.

The second awareness is even more fascinating. Know how to be satisfied with the things that we already have. When we think about this, we see that we truly have enough. We have this life. To some degree, we can say that the less we have, the more abundance we have. When we don't own anything at all, we have the abundance of the entire universe. This is the miracle of life, but instead we chase in vain after things. So wanting little and knowing how to be satisfied, we can be peaceful, can't we?

This principle of no gain applies to enlightenment, too. Since we are already it, we need not expect anything. This may be the most important attitude that we can take toward our practice or even our life. We can look at this from two aspects. One aspect is, "Don't expect anything." The other is, "Everything is already here!" What is there to expect? What else do you need? You have everything to begin with. *You don't need to become something or someone else!* You are already complete.

Buddha guarantees this to each of us with no exceptions. This is right understanding.

The last of the Eight Awarenesses is avoiding idle talk. These are, in effect, the last words of the Buddha's teaching. We can understand idle talk as the pursuit of conceptual thoughts or dualistic understanding. If we talk in dualistic ways, our talk becomes idle talk and we cannot have peace. We can even make our healthy body sick by our thoughts and vice versa. In our tradition, zazen is the best means to taste this nonduality, or peace. At the same time, practicing zazen to get something is not an ideal way to practice. Please do not expect any effects from zazen as such, just do zazen. Can you do this? In just doing zazen, zazen contributes to each of us, to the immediate sangha, to the extended sangha, and even further to the Three Treasures of Buddha, Dharma, and Sangha, which contain everything.

Please consider that your practice is not just for yourself. When you forget yourself, a transformation takes place. Then your life is no longer your life. It is the life of Buddha. Your practice is contributing much,

much more to others than you might think. If we must use any basic standard of evaluation, the fact that the life of each of us contains everything is the standard we should use. We make this realization clear through our practice. You are taking care of the dharma at the same time that the dharma is taking care of you.

So when you feel fear, pain, and frustration, appreciate your life as Buddha's life. Being sick, take good care of yourself instead of being upset and frustrated. Getting old? Enjoy it, Buddha is getting old. Have a feast with him! Why not? We have all had painful experiences. Turn your mind around and see how you can take it with the joy of Buddha. Just the way we look at these things can be the difference between heaven and hell. This is not to say there is not terrible suffering in life, but too often a tiny thing becomes a huge thing for us; it almost kills us. And yet, when we look at it from a different perspective, we laugh.

Clarify what life is, what death is. There is a very clear answer. How you appreciate it and how you live it is up to you. Please take care of it.

INTIMACY OF RELATIVE AND ABSOLUTE

INTIMACY IS ONE OF THE BASIC THEMES expressed in the poem *Identity of Relative and Absolute* written by Master Sekito Kisen, a Zen master in eighth-century China. The poem begins:

> *The mind of the Great Sage of India*
> *Is intimately conveyed West and East.*
> *Among human beings are wise ones and fools;*
> *In the Way there is no teacher of North and South.*

The implication of *identity* is not just that two things are one thing, but that there is the activity of being one. The two interact, and yet they are one. Being one is the activity of intimacy.

The first line is, "The mind of the Great Sage of India is intimately conveyed West and East." We use the word *conveyed,* but the word in Japanese is *mitsu,* or "intimacy." The mind of the Great Sage is intimate, not conveyed; it is here! Being intimate is this vivid, vital life itself. Be intimate with yourself! Buddha realized this intimacy and handed it down generation after generation, ancestor to ancestor, to us.

What is the relative and absolute? Master Sekito Kisen writes:

The relative fits the absolute as a box and its lid.
The absolute meets the relative
Like two arrows meeting in midair.

What is ordinary and what is absolute? Our ordinary life is the phenomenal or relative part; the fundamental, so-called essential nature, which is somewhat invisible to our physical eyes, is the absolute. Sometimes absolute, or *ri,* is translated as "principle, the primary point, or essential nature."

In the original Japanese version, this line literally means that when the relative exists, the box and its lid fit together. When the absolute responds to it, it is like two arrows meeting in midair. When the relative exists, the absolute responds to it like a box and its lid. It is like two arrows meeting in mid-air. Everyday life and essential nature—Buddha nature—are not separate.

Intimacy is also expressed in two arrows meeting in midair. How can two arrows meet in midair? It is almost impossible. And yet this is a very practical analogy.

The story of two arrows meeting in midair was originally expressed in *Reshi,* a book written more than two thousand years ago. There were two archery adepts, a teacher, Hiei, and a student, Kisho. Kisho was becoming more and more skillful and eventually he believed himself the best. Without his teacher Hiei, Kisho believed he would be the best in the world. One day, he tried to kill his teacher.

Kisho and Hiei happened to meet in a field when no one else was around. Kisho shot an arrow and his teacher, responding, shot back. The two arrows met in the air and fell to the ground. Kisho shot a second arrow and a third one. The same thing happened each time. But Hiei had only three arrows, and Kisho had four. He shot the fourth arrow, and the teacher automatically picked a branch with thorns from a bush and stopped that arrow with the thorn. You may think such a thing is impossible, yet at the same time, can you take it as an analogy for your life?

Our essential nature, our Buddha nature, and all the different manifestations of our world are not two. Subject and object are altogether as one. As an individual, your so-called true self and your so-called apparent self are not separate. Our true life and our daily life are not separate. All our surroundings and this self are not separate. The point is how do we see it? Do we see it as one?

Just seeing this is not enough. We must ask how our daily life *functions* as the life of everything. How are these two arrows meeting? If we say it is impossible for two arrows to meet in midair, we can say that it is also impossible for each one of us to meet all external phenomena as one, right here, right now. So how do they meet? Or rather, how to live so that this life and all externals are together intimate as your own life? You cannot do this by any intellectual efforts or schemes, for when you do you encounter this *I, my, me*.

Intimacy is nothing but realizing the fact that already you are *as you are*. Your essential nature is nothing but you as you are. See that these two arrows already meeting is your own life. You are no longer whatever you think you are, you yourself are the life of the dharma, the life of Buddha. Realizing this fact is the moment of transmission. Transmission from whom to whom? There is nothing to be transmitted from anybody else to you, not even your true Self. This is intimacy. How do you appreciate it?

There is a koan in the *Transmission of the Light** about being intimate. The forty-second patriarch Ryozan Enkan was attending his teacher Doan Zenji. The patriarch Doan asked him, "What is that beneath your robe?" In other words, "Who are you?" Ryozan had no answer. Doan

* The following koan is adapted from Francis H. Cook, trans., *The Record of Transmitting the Light: Zen Master Keizan's Denkoroku* (Los Angeles: Center Publications, 1991), 190.

Zenji said, "It is the most painful thing when one who studies the Buddha Way hasn't yet reached that stage. Now you ask me." So Ryozan asked, "What is that beneath your robe?" The patriarch Doan replied, "Intimacy." Ryozan was greatly awakened.

Taking refuge in the Three Treasures is also intimacy. I am not talking about anything special. Be one with the Buddha. Be one with the Dharma. Be one with the Sangha. The Sangha meets when the Buddha arrow and the Dharma arrow meet. Where do they meet? Right here, now, as our life, as my life! This very moment is midair! The Buddha, the unsurpassable Way, is absolute. So if we call it darkness, it is dark; if we say it is a subtle source, it is a subtle source. All appearances as light and dark, clear, muddy, messy, transparent, appearing and disappearing, and so on, are all the dharma.

Really be intimate with no division between yourself and others. Then everything becomes nothing but you. Nothing could be more intimate than this. This is the buddhas' teaching, your original self. You cannot separate your life from Buddha.

Of course, the two arrows meeting in midair is an analogy, and analogies never cover every aspect. This analogy simply indicates the fact of truly being one. So in daily life, please accept yourself as you are—as absolute, as the source—and accept your life as it is, as male or female, young or old, smart or dull. Given this fact of absolute and relative, we are all the same and we are all different, each having our own unique function and position. Whether you see these two arrows meeting in midair as difficult or easy, see it as the ease and difficulty of your own life.

Trust yourself as you truly are; you are already the Buddha Way itself. Be intimate with it. Do not make yourself separate with your opinions, your judgments, your ideas, with whatever you think your life is. When you do that, the two arrows miss each other. If there is any difficulty, it is simply the difficulty of how to be intimate with yourself.

The two arrows meeting is the mind of the sage and the ordinary mind. Our ordinary life is intimate to begin with, but unfortunately we experience our everyday life as a split life, as if the enlightened life is separate from it. So this identity is of oneself and Oneself and of Oneself and others. Others are not necessarily just human beings. How to be intimate with Oneself and the phenomenal world? This fact has been transmitted down to us. How you take care of it is your responsibility.

In your daily life, please accept yourself as you are and appreciate your life as it is. Be intimate with yourself. Taking good care of yourself is always the best way to take care of everything. Then your life, I am sure, will go all right. I want you to be a truly intimate being. Beneath your robe is the same as outside your robe. Inside and outside the robe are one. There is no division. Please take good care of this life. Enjoy yourself!

CLARIFY THE GREAT MATTER

Once while in China, I was reading a collection of sayings by an ancient master. At the time, a monk from Sichuan, a sincere practitioner of the Way, asked me, "What is the use of reading recorded sayings?" I replied, "I want to learn about the deeds of the ancient masters." The monk asked, "What is the use of that?" I said, "I wish to teach people after I return home." The monk queried further, "Yes, but ultimately, what is the use?"

Later, I pondered his remarks. Learning the deeds of the ancient masters by reading the recorded sayings or koans in order to explain them to deluded people is ultimately of no use to my own practice or for teaching others. Even if I don't know a single letter, I will be able to show it to others in inexhaustible ways if I devote myself to just sitting and clarifying the great matter. It was for this reason that the monk pressed me as to the ultimate use [of reading and studying]. I thought what he said was true. Thereupon, I gave up reading the recorded sayings and other texts, concentrated wholeheartedly on sitting, and was able to clarify the great matter.

—*Eihei Dogen,*
SHOBOGENZO ZUIMONKI

Some people think that our practice in the Soto tradition is just-sitting. I feel fortunate that I had a chance to study koans. In this passage Dogen Zenji does not say just sit. What is the difference between physically sitting on a cushion and sitting in shikantaza? *Shikantaza* is often translated as "just sit!" *Shikan* means "wholeheartedly" or "just," *za* is the verb "to sit," and *ta* is an emphatic, an exclamation point. Even to concentrate on sitting wholeheartedly is not enough. Dogen Zenji does not say just wholeheartedly sit on a cushion. If you believe in just doing that, place a rock or a piece of wood on a cushion and let it sit. It sits better than we do. Is that enlightened life? We should not fool ourselves.

Some of you ask, "What am I supposed to do during zazen? Should I just be aware of what is going on around me and observe carefully?" Let's look at *shikan* once more. Dogen Zenji emphasizes the *shi* part. What is *shi*? Stop! Stop the conscious mind from going on and on and on and on, from one subject to another, unceasingly. And *kan* means seeing, observing, or being aware. These may seem contradictory, but both are important, do you see? If you can stop the conscious mind from going on and on, then you can be aware of what is truly going on, what to do, and how to do it.

In *Shobogenzo Bendowa,* Dogen Zenji talks about the content of shikantaza and about clarifying this great matter. He uses this expression, "clarifying this great matter," twice even in this short passage. What is the great matter? This is the koan. The *Lotus Sutra* also asks, "Why do buddhas appear in the world? It is because of this one grave, important matter." The great matter is your true life. Is there a false life? It is your true self. Is there any false self? Is your life a fake? It cannot be. Is your life true? How is it true? This is the great matter: how to clarify your life. In a way, this has nothing to do with sitting. But so far, zazen has proven to be the best and surest way to clarify it.

Shakyamuni Buddha guarantees us that we all have the wisdom and the virtuous aspects of the Tathagata Buddha. What does this mean? This is the great matter! Clarify it and see it as the treasury of the true dharma eye and subtle mind of nirvana. Confirm for yourself that the wisdom and virtue you have are the same as the Buddha's. When your zazen becomes the zazen of Tathagata Buddha, then you are doing shikantaza. Otherwise you are doing something else.

Dogen Zenji says that reading is unnecessary, even studying is unnecessary. In fact, any kind of practice is unnecessary. He says just sit and clarify this great matter. He does not say that we should not study. He himself studied many things. It is said that he read the entire Tripitaka, a collection of early Buddhist texts, three times through. We can all benefit from study, but at certain periods of time it may be wise not to read much. This is what Dogen Zenji is talking about here.

You might feel that being Christian could be a hindrance to practice, or being a woman, a monk, a layperson, being young or old, smart or dull. These might become hindrances as much as reading literature or poetry or the sayings of the masters. Ultimately, it does not matter whether you are Jewish, Christian, European, American, yellow, white, or black, whether you read or don't read. Buddha himself was Hindu. As a Hindu, he became buddha. Buddha wants you to become buddha, awake, whether you're Jewish, Catholic, or Protestant, whether reading or not reading. Why not?

Do you see the problem? You say, "I am doing shikantaza." No, you are not. This is the problem. You say, "I am working on koan." No, you are not. As soon as you objectify it, as soon as there is any separation between you and shikantaza, between you and koan, there is the problem. Reading books is not the way to solve the problem. Not reading books is not the way to solve the problem. It has nothing to do with working on koan or not working on koan, with doing shikantaza or not doing shikantaza. If you say it does, then you should truly practice koan or truly practice shikantaza. *Shikan* is the koan; *taza* is the case. Koan and shikantaza are the same. We should not be blinded by words. Realize the grave matter! Integrate it! This is why the buddhas appear.

Clarifying the grave matter is more important than simply reading the sayings of the masters. Rather, we should deal with koans, which are the sayings of the old masters, in such a way that our life is one of great intimacy, of shikan. In that way our life will be the same as the sayings and doings of the masters. The masters' sayings manifest as the realization of our lives. This is how we should deal with koans and with shikantaza. How you do it and how much you do it is your practice. And along with your practice, the realization of your life manifests. Your life is nothing but the Way.

This so-called realization or enlightenment is not something that you add to yourself; it is not something outside your life. It already is your life. It is also the life of Shakyamuni Buddha himself and of all the masters, including Dogen Zenji. When we realize this, we will see ourselves hand in hand with all the masters. And furthermore, my life, your life, becomes the life of the buddhas and ancestors. This is the transmission. That is the meaning of shikantaza and the meaning of koan. Realize it! Your life is already this fact. Shakyamuni Buddha's enlightenment guarantees it.

SAVE ALL SENTIENT BEINGS

THE FOUR BODHISATTVA VOWS

Sentient beings are numberless, I vow to save them;
Desires are inexhaustible, I vow to put an end to them;
The dharmas are boundless, I vow to master them;
The Buddha Way is unsurpassable, I vow to attain it.

WHEN I REFLECT UPON THE VOW of saving all sentient beings, I am actually reflecting about saving myself. Saving oneself is the fulfillment of the vow to save all sentient beings. *Oneself* has a double implication. The first refers to this limited self, this individual life; the second refers to Oneself, this whole life as One. This expresses the very basic premise of Buddha's teaching: one is all, all is one. One Mind is all dharma, everything. This One Mind, body and mind, is anything, everything.

We usually divide our life into two. There is usually me and my life, and then there is some other life that is separate from me, or not-me. But in fact, this is not so; there is no other life that is separate from you. When you live your life in this separate way, the vow to save all sentient beings becomes nonsense.

How can I save all sentient beings? The bodhisattva is one with the Way, one with bodhi. *Sattva* is "person" and *bodhi* is "enlightenment," or realization of the Way. So to some degree the bodhisattva is the one who truly realizes and understands what the Way is, what life is, and then just lives that life.

We have another general definition of bodhisattva as the one who, instead of taking care of herself, does something for others. For the bodhisattva, self and other are the same. In doing for others, the bodhisattva knows that he is doing for himself, too.

How do we save all sentient beings? We say that the bodhisattva's job is selling water by the river. Isn't this unnecessary? There is plenty of water in the river for everyone. In fact, we are the water itself, true nature itself! No one needs to buy it. But we don't believe that our life is the Way *just as it is*.

We also have a saying: In order to take care of poison, use poison. A bodhisattva uses everything, including intellectual ideas and discriminative thinking, in order to save all sentient beings from their attachment to their ideas and discriminative thinking.

The bodhisattva does all these things in order to take care of certain situations. In a sense, you live in a dualistic way because you are confused and do not trust yourself, and for this reason the bodhisattva has to sell water by the river. But duality itself is also absolute. So are the bodhisattva's actions. We talk about things as if one thing is relative and another is absolute, but in fact, there is no such thing as absolute or relative. Such distinctions exist only in our thoughts.

So when we have pain or struggles, our suffering itself is absolute. All our actions are absolute. But when we *talk* about something as being absolute, then it is relative to something else. This is not the absolute; it is just an idea. Ideas are always relative, dualistic in subject and object, in opposition to this *I*, *my*, *me*.

Who is the bodhisattva? Each of us is the bodhisattva. And each moment of our life includes all sentient beings. This was the starting point for Shakyamuni Buddha. When he attained Buddhahood, he exclaimed, "I and the great earth, all beings, have simultaneously attained the Way." Can you see the relationship between Shakyamuni's *I* and *all beings?* Does *I* attain the Way simultaneously with all beings, or do all beings simultaneously attain the Way with *I?* The bodhisattva's vow to save all beings is vowing to realize what this *I* is. This is our practice. Regardless of whether we realize it or not, our life is this *one is all, all is one*. Realization is nothing other than becoming aware of this fact.

So this general vow of the bodhisattva can be examined literally as well as from different perspectives. We should closely examine who the bodhisattva is and what bodhi is. What is meant by all beings and by *I?* This *I* is always the key point. "I and the great earth, all beings." Are these separate or one? And how do we all accomplish the Way simultaneously? This is the task of the bodhisattva; this is our vow.

The next vow is: *Desires are inexhaustible, I vow to put an end to them.* Dharmas, all phenomena, are also inexhaustible, so in a sense, desires and dharmas are not much different. As a matter of fact, these desires also include the bodhisattva's desires to save all beings, and in doing so, he himself or she herself is saved. This is a greedy desire. Usually we think that we should not have desires, that they are somehow bad. *Bon no,* which we translate as "desires," is also "caring." We care about all sorts of things, and there are different kinds of caring.

On a commonsense level, if your caring is right caring, then do it. If it is wrong caring, then stop it. What makes it right or wrong caring? We come back to separation, duality. If we do not see things as one, we fall into the dichotomy that creates the relative world, the right and wrong, the good and bad. Then caring is no longer true caring. When our caring is creating the problem, it should be cut off. So in other words, in seeing the whole, in seeing everything as one life, we eliminate the desires or the causes for our troubles; we eliminate the deluded life.

We have all kinds of dharma principles. In koan study the Five Ranks of Master Tozan* express the state of oneness from five different per-

* The teachings of Master Tozan, or Tung Shan, the cofounder of Soto Zen in China in the tenth century—Eds.

spectives. In the Ten Ox-Herding Pictures,† our life is seen from ten perspectives. In other words, this one life is appreciated from many different perspectives. This leads to the third vow: *The dharmas are boundless, I vow to master them*. It is always one dharma, and this one dharma is boundless. Indeed it is! It is not one, three, or ten, but literally anything, everything. It is the life of each of us! How do we master these dharmas? The way to master them is to truly see what this life is. The Buddha Way, the enlightened Way, or the life of the bodhisattva is the best way. *The Buddha Way is unsurpassable, I vow to attain it*. So let us realize the Way together. This is the fourth vow.

Our life is the Way to begin with. So who is the bodhisattva? Having abundant water as your life, who needs to buy water? Just be yourself as the Way itself. This is the best way to be a bodhisattva, living this seemingly small individual life in relationship to all surroundings as the mutual exchange of energy, as a whole, as one life.

One of you said to me, "I know my life is wrong." When I heard this, I thought that this person must have a very clear understanding! Usually we do not realize that our life is not quite right. And this person said further, "I know my life is wrong because I am so selfish." So he knows the reason, too! This is a wonderful place to start. He knows that discriminating between *I* and *other* creates problems. Unfortunately, we all do this and so we invite the problems of separation. It is easy to talk about this, but how do we actually take care of it?

I quite often recall the koan "Zuigan's Master." My father also loved this koan. I believe it was a guideline for him. When I was very little, I vividly remember my father speaking to my brothers and me about this koan. It was a good lesson. Master Zuigan calls to himself, "Is the master in? Is the master in?" And Zuigan answers himself, "Yes, I am." And Zuigan asks further, "Are you really awake?" Then he answers himself, "Yes, I am." Then Zuigan says, "Do not be deceived by others." Zuigan replies, "No, I won't."

This is a marvelous koan. My father asked us, "Who are the others?"

† A series of ten pictures originally created by a twelfth-century Chinese Zen master depicting the various stages of Zen practice and realization—Eds.

From time to time we complain about all kinds of things about other people, and we feel that we are being deceived. My father told us that these others are not living outside ourselves. The more I reflect on this teaching, it has double, even triple meanings. Just an amazing thing, those others inside myself. How true it is!

There should not be divisions. Everything is always happening now. We may feel that something happens in the future, but in fact, each moment is now. We may realize certain things more distinctly in certain moments, but it is always *now*. When we do not see this, when we create divisions, we are this much deluded.

Please really appreciate yourself! This life of each of us is most precious. If you disagree, you are the one who must buy water by the river. This is a very clear-cut, straightforward issue. How can we realize this fact of our life and live it?

KOANS OF ZAZEN

DOGEN ZENJI'S *Universal Promotion of the Principles of Zazen** is a fundamental text relating to the practice of zazen. The Soto master Harada Sogaku Roshi picked certain phrases from this text and worked with them as koans.

For me there is basically no difference between koan and zazen. What is the most important point of both koan and zazen? Needless to say, it is our life. We call our life Buddha nature. Mountains and rivers and the great earth all depend on this nature. Strictly speaking, everything is no other than this nature. What is this Buddha nature? It is the absoluteness of life, it is our life. This is what all the masters in different times and places have dealt with. And now that is what you are dealing with, too. This boundless life is the true life of each of us, do you see?

How can zazen be practiced by anybody, everybody? How can koan

* Waddell and Abe, 13–16.

be practiced in this way? A koan is not solving a puzzle or playing some kind of game. No! What is important is how you are taking care of your life. Sometimes this life is a shit stick, sometimes a true man of no rank, sometimes a wheel, a dog, a cat, trees, flowers, mountains and rivers, and the great earth. All of these appear as Buddha nature.

The first koan that Harada Roshi picked from this *Universal Promotion of the Principles of Zazen* is, "The Way is basically perfect and all-pervading." And it goes with the next line, "The dharma vehicle is free and untrammeled." What is the dharma vehicle? How does it function freely? How can we appreciate life as perfect and all-pervading? We say that life is a manifestation of one thing, and it is also a manifestation of everything. That is also the nature of *our* life. It has no limit, it is free and untrammeled. If we think we are limited, we think so in our head. This life is limitless!

The second koan is, "If there is the slightest discrepancy, the Way is as distant as heaven from earth." Dogen Zenji says later on, "When you take one misstep, right there you fail." This is true, isn't it? In order to go somewhere, if you go in even a slightly different direction, the distance becomes wider and wider the farther you go. So we should be careful about even the slightest discrepancy. Relating to our zazen, what creates this discrepancy? How does this discrepancy arise? This is a most important point to consider, especially because of how much trouble this discrepancy causes us.

The third koan is, "One is making the initial, partial excursions about the frontiers." What are these "initial, partial excursions"? Then along with that line, "It is still somewhat deficient in the vital Way of total emancipation." What is the Way of total emancipation? What is the relationship between partial excursions and total emancipation?

Then the fourth koan. "Learn the backward step that turns your light inwardly to illuminate yourself." What does this mean? I do not mean as an explanation, but actually, as a matter of *fact,* how do you illuminate yourself inwardly, and how do you step backward? How do you look at yourself?

The next koan follows: When you take that backward step, then "body and mind of themselves will drop away and your original face will be manifest." How does your original face manifest? How does your body and mind drop away? Isn't it a wonderful koan? I am quoting exactly what Dogen Zenji says. Each sentence is a beautiful koan.

What is this original face? In Buddhism we do not separate the essence from the appearance or reality. The intrinsic nature and relative reality of this body all together are Buddha nature, the original face. This very flimsy, clumsy life itself is none other than Buddha nature, do you see?

What is prior to all our intellectual knowledge and discriminative functions of our mind? There is a famous koan of the Sixth Patriarch Hui-neng, who was an illiterate newcomer to the monastery but his realization was profound. Much to the shock of the monks who had practiced long and hard at the monastery, he was recognized by the Fifth Patriarch as his dharma heir. So when Hui-neng received dharma transmission from the Fifth Patriarch, his life was in danger, and he went into hiding in the mountains. Monk Myo, a former general, chased after him. When Myo caught up with him, the Sixth Patriarch said, "Without thinking good or evil, show me your original face." In other words, prior to this or that, prior to right or wrong, good or bad, prior to all these discursive thoughts, what is there? What is the original face? What is *your* original face?

The sixth koan is how to sit. Dogen Zenji says, "Think of not-thinking. How do you think of not-thinking? Nonthinking. This is in itself the essential art of zazen." This refers to a famous koan by Master Yakusan Igen. A monk asks Master Yakusan, "When we do zazen, what do we think about?" We have the same question, don't we? When we sit, how do we think about sitting? Master Yakusan says, "Think of the unthinkable." In other words, think of not-thinking, or no-thinking. The monk's question naturally follows: "How can we think of not-thinking?" Or of the unthinkable, or no-thinking? Master Yakusan replies, "Nonthinking."

We could penetrate this essence of zazen endlessly. What is non-thinking? Think without thinking! Sit without sitting. What kind of thinking is this? What kind of zazen is this? Or, what is the thinking of zazen? What does zazen think when zazen is doing zazen?

Dogen Zenji tells you to really drop body and mind. This is the most important way to do zazen. What is he talking about? And what is the difference between koan and zazen in dropping body and mind? Maintain this one Buddha-mind seal. What is this Buddha-mind seal? I say it's koan. It's shikantaza. It's *shobogenzo,* the treasury of the true dharma eye and subtle mind of nirvana. And how to maintain this one Buddha-mind seal is our practice, our life! Our vows, our aspirations, are to truly maintain this Buddha-mind seal. Do not let this torch die out!

The next koan is: "Practice-realization is naturally undefiled." This is obvious. When you do this kind of zazen, there is no defilement. In fact, there is no such thing as practice or realization, as such. Dogen Zenji says further, "Going forward in practice is a matter of everydayness." Regardless of how far you go in practice-realization, it is ordinary, it is not anything special. In other words, it does not matter whether this is your first zazen, or zazen of ten years, fifty years, it is just ordinary life. So how is that practice-realization not defiled?

The last koan is, "Your treasure store will open of itself and you will use it at will." How does your treasure house open by itself? How do you appreciate it and use it?

Isn't this something? Every sentence has beautiful, marvelous points that we can work with carefully as koans, as guides for our life. I encourage you to read the *Universal Promotion of the Principles of Zazen* at least once a day; digest it well, even memorize it. Then penetrate it, touch the heart of what Dogen Zenji is saying. What kind of zazen does he want us to do? And when we do such zazen, Dogen Zenji says body and mind naturally drop off and our original face manifests. In other words, our true life will manifest by itself.

I WANT TO SHARE WITH YOU my experience during a Zen and Christian Life worship service. We chanted Buddhist sutras and each person also read a passage from the Beatitudes. The passage I happened to read was, "Blessed are the pure in heart for they shall see God." I had heard this passage before, but it made a very strong impression upon me this time. What does it mean, to be pure in heart? This is a wonderful koan.

What does *heart* mean? It definitely does not mean our physical hearts. Heart is simply heart. *Mind,* a key term in Buddhism, is a synonym for the same thing. The Beatitudes also speak of spirit: "Blessed are the poor in spirit." Do you distinguish between spirit, heart, and mind? I do not.

Of course, we can make up definitions, but these definitions will not reveal the true meaning of spirit, heart, or mind. In the *Heart Sutra,* or *Hannya Shingyo, shin* literally means "mind." It also has another implication, which is "center." *Spirit* also has many implications. If you were asked to define what spirit is, I am sure all of you would say different things.

At one extreme in our tradition, we say *mushin,* no-mind. At the other extreme, we say everything is *shin,* mind. Are that one mind and no-mind the same mind or different? If you say different, what is the difference? If you say the same, how is it the same? When we say body and mind, is that mind the same as no-mind, as one mind, as my mind, your mind?

"Blessed are the pure in heart." What is heart? I feel that this heart must be the heart of God. Blessed is the one who is genuine enough to be in the heart of God. The Beatitude actually says, "They shall see God." This is very interesting!

"They shall see God." What does it mean? What is God? You might have a definition, but that is a definition, not God. We have a similar saying about seeing the Tathagata. "When you try to see the Tathagata with the forms, you won't see him." Form is the object of our senses, our perceptions. So how can you see God? Do you realize that everything you see is God?

We could rephrase it, "Blessed are the pure in heart for they shall see the Buddha," or "they shall see the dharma." Consider what Dogen Zenji says about the Dharma Treasure. He says that the Dharma Treasure is pure and genuine, apart from dust.

When you see the dharma, you see the purity. When you are pure in heart, I am sure you also see the dharma. However, if you think to yourself, "I am pure," to that degree you are still stained. That is because you hold on to your ideas about what is pure and what is not pure. You are comparing something that you think is pure with what you think is defiled. In other words, the relative is not truly pure. When you are pure in heart, when you do not hold on to such ideas and do not make comparisons, you see God, you see Buddha.

What is this defilement that is the opposite of purity? What defiles our hearts? "Blessed are the poor in spirit, for theirs is the kingdom of heaven." We have almost the same teaching in Buddhism. "Blessed are the poor in spirit, for theirs is the Lotus Land." Isn't it beautiful?

What does *poor* mean? Usually we say that having less than the average amount may be called poor. But what does it mean to be poor in spirit? We can say it means to have nothing in spirit. Nothing in spirit, nothing in mind, no-mind, no spirit. Then what remains? Just as it says: "the kingdom of heaven." What a beautiful way to say it!

Usually we think of heaven as something limited, but these days even scientists are finding that the universe is constantly expanding. Can you imagine? It has no end. It is literally boundless. The kingdom of heaven literally means the kingdom of no limit. Boundlessness! No-mind, or we can say one mind. Everything is literally boundless, limitless. That is poor!

In Case 10 of the *Gateless Gate,** monk Seizei begs Master Sozan, "I am poor and destitute. Please give me something." Of course, Seizei is not literally begging for food or money. "I have nothing," he says, "do you have something to give me?" And Master Sozan answers, "You have

* *The Mumonkan*, a famous collection of Zen koans—Eds.

drunk three cups of the best wine, and still you say that your lips are not yet moistened." There is a beautiful connection between this koan and the Beatitudes. How can you be poor in spirit? The kingdom of God is in your heart. What does this mean?

For me, these Beatitudes are truly wonderful koans. Of course, we can say very superficially that in Christianity there is the dichotomy between creator and creation, but I do not agree. If you appreciate it only in this way, then you, like monk Seizei, are the one who will never be completely satisfied. I am sure of this. Maybe this is why some of you are doing Zen practice. If so, I guarantee that as long as you are in this frame of mind, you will not get much out of Zen practice, either.

See this purity. Be pure in heart. And if you truly want to realize the Lotus Land, be poor in spirit. How do you see the Way, the Lotus Land? How do you see the kingdom of heaven or see God? As Dogen Zenji says, "Forget the self." This is the way to be pure. Drop off body and mind. This is the way to be poor. Christ says poor in spirit. Dogen Zenji repeatedly emphasizes that body and mind are not two separate things. When you say, "I am poor," you are still carrying something. If you say, "I am genuine" or "I am pure," to that degree something is still attached. So truly drop off body and mind, really forget the self.

Our very nature is poverty. We call this no-mind. Genuineness and purity, this is our nature. When you are really pure in heart, I am sure you will see your true nature. That is what each one of us should clearly experience. In a way we are doing it, but we must clarify the difference between the life that breathes and is alive at this very moment, and our thoughts of what and how it is. When we are truly humble, thoroughly surrendering to the dharma, then we are able to be poor, to be pure.

In our tradition, our practice focuses on this point. When you see the no-mind that is poor in spirit and when you see the no-nature that is pure in heart, surely you see the Buddha. That is your true nature, the best Way. If you do not experience this for yourself, it does not matter whether you are Christian or Buddhist, you will struggle with yourself.

As a human being, what is the difference between you and me or between Buddhist and Christian? Even among Buddhists and among

Christians there are different approaches. But what we appreciate should not be different, however we express it. If we can selflessly experience the existence of God, I am sure we will know the Savior.

So it seems to me that we should be aware of how each one of us, as an individual, can literally be pure in heart. How can we be poor in spirit, humble? When we suffer, what really causes our pain? There is separation, alienation. Why does it happen? Because we are not poor, we are not humble, we are not pure. When you take care of this, it is what we call *kensho,* seeing God, realizing the kingdom in your heart as the place where you live. This is the Lotus Land.

Of course, just seeing this is not enough. You must live that life. When we have difficulties or troubles, peace of mind is not something that comes from outside, but something you find inside yourself. How can we open up this limitless life and extend this boundless land? This is our practice.

COPYING SUTRAS

WHAT IS THE PRACTICE of copying sutras? The *Lotus Sutra* says repeatedly that those who copy the *Lotus Sutra* will accomplish supreme enlightenment. Copying is an excellent way to put yourself fully into a sutra. You are one with copying and one with the sutra, truly sensing and feeling it. The action and object are easily unified. When you are copying, there is a sense of copying and also of the sutra allowing you to copy it. The sutra is copying you, too! This interrelationship is felt intimately, and such a state of being is itself supreme enlightenment.

Which sutra should you copy? You can copy any sutra or even part of a long one. Copying the *Heart Sutra* is a very common practice in Japan these days. Of course this is copied in Chinese, but there is no reason for you not to copy the sutra in English. There are different ways to copy a sutra. Some people copy one stroke or one word, do three bows, sit down, write another stroke or word, and then do three bows again. Others write one character or one word, then make a bow. Others simply copy. However you express your respect toward the sutra, please do it with sincere devotion and reverence.

In his writings on the *Lotus Sutra,* Dogen Zenji wrote of the lotus as the blossom of the subtle dharma. The lotus is a very unusual flower. Do you know its unique characteristics? When a lotus blooms, the seeds grow together with the flower. Usually a flower blossoms and after that turns into seed. But not so with the lotus. It is amazing. When the lotus blooms, big lotus seeds are already growing in the bottom of the flower.

Consider these seeds and flower as an analogy for our life and its blossoming. If we say that the major part of our life extends for twenty, forty, or fifty years, that period could be called the flowering. But the result, or the seed, does not necessarily come after the flowering as such. It exists *now* within our life; it is always existing. The result is already here with us!

Another characteristic of the lotus is that it grows in the mud and yet is not defiled. At the end of our meals, we chant: "May we exist in muddy water with purity like a lotus, thus we bow to Buddha." This is a good translation, but there is another translation that makes a different point. Chinese is a very rich language. The same words are pronounced in a different way according to the different dynasties. Personally, I like to chant this verse with the T'ang dynasty pronunciation instead of how we do it in Japanese, which is more like the Han dynasty pronunciation.

Using the T'ang dynasty pronunciation, this verse can also mean: "May we live in the world with purity like a lotus." While living in the world, live like the lotus flower, not attached to the water or the mud. When water drops on the lotus leaf, the water rolls off right away. The analogy for us is to live like the water droplet, not attaching anywhere. So consider both implications, that of being pure and genuine, and at the same time that of being free. Not being attached, the mind is kept in a pure and free way.

What does the lotus flower stand for? The subtle dharma. We chant the "Gatha on Opening the Sutra" before every talk in the zendo:

The dharma, incomparably profound and infinitely subtle,
Is rarely encountered even in millions of ages.

Now we see it, hear it, receive and maintain it.
May we completely realize the Tathagata's true meaning.

That subtle dharma is this subtle dharma of the lotus blossom. How do you receive it? How do you maintain it? Living this subtle dharma every day, how do you see it? When chanting, we experience it. When reading, we experience it. When writing and copying, we experience it. What are we truly copying? We can say that I am literally writing my life through copying this most precious subtle dharma.

So what is truly the sutra? And how do you truly read or copy the sutra? How do you see it, hear it, and maintain it *now* as the subtle dharma? The sutra must be alive as the functioning of your life! Please trust yourself. Trust in yourself as the sutra, as the dynamic, boundless dharma itself. This is what I mean when I say be nice to yourself. Trusting your life as the sutra is the best way to be nice to yourself.

This practice of sutra copying has wonderful merit. I encourage you to do it and enjoy it. By copying, you will enrich your life, and you will experience yourself being revolved by the sutra. Unify yourself with what you do! This is actually the key, this unity of your true life and the life of literally everything. Do you see?

PART THREE

Where Is
the Hindrance?

Where Is the Hindrance?

OUR LIFE IS USUALLY SO HECTIC that we quite easily lose ourselves. Zazen is a wonderful opportunity to face and closely study ourselves. In a way, it is almost a joke to have to find out who we are or to
realize what our life is. Our life, this life, is already in realization. It is
already manifesting, so what is there to look for? When we look for
something, Buddha calls this delusion. Unfortunately, this is what all of
us do in one way or another.

There is an interesting koan in the *Blue Cliff Record,* a dialogue between Master Kyosei and a monk. The monk asks, "I want to peck from
the inside. Would you please tap from the outside?" When an egg is
ready to hatch, the chick inside pecks at the shell. The mother hen
senses it and taps on the outside. When it is time, just a little tap on the
outside breaks the shell and the chick hatches. If the shell breaks too
soon or too late, the chick dies. So the monk said, "Please tap from the
outside." Master Kyosei asks, "Will you be alive?" The monk answers,
"If not, I'll be ridiculed." Master Kosei replies, "You also are one of
those in the weeds."

What is the point of this koan? "I am ready, please let me come out." Where is the shell? Where is the hindrance? What is keeping you imprisoned? There is an expression in Japanese, "Without a rope, people bind themselves." You do not think you are completely free, so you practice trying to liberate yourself. But what is binding you? Look around you. Nothing is binding you, and yet you cannot see it. You feel as if you are bound by something. Buddha calls this delusion. Your mind is not in the right place.

In our practice we hold sesshin, an intensive Zen retreat. *Sesshin* means to join or unify the mind. It can also mean to put the mind in the place where the mind belongs. Of course the mind is already unified or in the right place, but nevertheless, we practice in this way. How do you put your mind in the right place? Where is the right place? *Right here* is always the place. This place or space of right here extends endlessly throughout the ten directions, the whole universe. This limited place of right here becomes universal, the existence of the cosmos. It is not limited to a particular race, culture, or country. And *right now* is the time. The infinite time span from past to future is reduced to this very moment, right now! Vice versa is also true. The moment of right now contains all the beginningless past and the endless future. It is universal.

For instance, one of the most important dharmas is the law of causation, of cause and effect. Everything is the cause of something and the effect of something. So in one way or another, everything is connected. The Japanese word for "karma" is *innen*. *In* is a direct cause or causes, and *nen* is an indirect cause or causes. All of these direct and indirect causes are present for each action.

We say "cause and effect are not two separate things" or "cause and effect are one." For example, when the teacher rings the bell, the student goes to *dokusan,* or interview. The conventional way of seeing this is that the ringing of the bell is the cause, and the effect is that the student goes into the dokusan room. But in Zen we say that the world is completely interconnected, that everything happens right here, right now. So the student goes into the dokusan room not just because the bell has been rung but because of all actions—not just actions in the past but actions in the present and future, too, because time is just a mental concept. Everything we do affects everything in the world. For this reason, none of us can do anything just by ourselves. Think of all the direct and the indirect causes that have influenced us.

So the action of the student entering the dokusan room includes the ringing of the bell. But the ringing of the bell also includes the action of the student going into the room. That is what we mean when we say that cause and effect are one. Every action is complete in each moment as both cause and effect, for each action is both the cause of other things and the effect of other things.

In a way, right here and right now, space and time, are all abstractions. What makes space and time real? You, your very being as you are gives space and time significance. It is easy for us to understand that without space and time we cannot survive. The reverse is also true. Without our very being, no space, no time, no history, and no world exist. In other words, our very life itself is the process of the creation of the world, of everything.

This is what I mean when I tell you all the time to take good care of yourself, according to the position you have and the work that needs to be done. In doing so, you extend your practice into your daily life, unifying everything as is. If this is not happening, then make this your practice. Nothing is binding you. If you feel that something is binding you, what is it? How do you take care of it?

Please have deep conviction and trust in yourself to be truly Yourself. There is no other way. By doing so, you will have a very deep confidence and respect for yourself. Going one step further, since the life of each of us contains everything, taking care of yourself is taking care of everything else, do you see?

SEE THE SHADOW
OF THE WHIP

THERE IS A FASCICLE in Dogen Zenji's *Shobogenzo* entitled "Shobo-genzo Shime [Four Horses]." He begins this fascicle with the famous case 32 from the *Gateless Gate*, The Non-Buddhist Questions the Buddha:

> One day a nonbeliever visiting Shakyamuni Buddha said, "Question with or without words?" And Buddha remained silent. Then after some time the nonbeliever prostrated before the Buddha and said, "Because of your great compassionate teaching, I am relieved of all illusion and see the Buddhist Way clearly before me." He again prostrated before Shakyamuni and left. After this departure, Honorable Ananda questioned the Buddha, "What did the nonbeliever find that caused him to perceive the Way?" And Venerable Shakyamuni replied, "A good horse is one that runs merely on seeing the shadow of a whip."*

What is being expressed here with and without words? As you know, our life itself is expressed. In a way all of you know what life is, and yet at the same time you have an uncertain feeling about it, don't you?

The non-Buddhist, not sitting even one period of zazen, goes to Shakyamuni Buddha and asks, "With words, without words?" What is the non-Buddhist asking? And what did the Buddha do? Shakyamuni Buddha sat there, not saying anything. The non-Buddhist appreciated the Buddha, said thanks, and left. Who is the non-Buddhist? Many of you are Judeo-Christian. Even those who have received the Buddhist precepts are Jewish or Christian to some degree. So what did this non-Buddhist realize?

Although the Buddha was silent to the non-Buddhist, he spoke to Ananda. What is the Buddha telling Ananda about the non-Buddhist and

* Kosen Nishiyama, trans., *Shobogenzo*, vol. 3 (Tokyo: Nakayama Shobo, 1983), 112.

the horse? When you are sensitive enough, you can feel the whip of Shakyamuni Buddha. Who is he whipping? Is it Ananda? Or you?

The teaching of this koan has to do with the importance of awakening. The non-Buddhist is asking, "What kind of way is with words, without words?" Dogen Zenji clearly states it is the unsurpassable, the very best Way. He quotes from the *Agama Sutra:*

> The Buddha said to the assembled people: "There are four kinds
> of horses. The first is a horse that out of fear will obey his rider's
> will at the mere sight of the whip's shadow. The second will act
> accordingly when the whip touches its hair. The third, when the
> whip has struck its flesh. And the fourth will yield only when
> the whip has reached its very bones. The first horse is like a man
> who realizes impermanence when he learns of a death in the
> neighboring village. The second horse is like a man who realizes
> this when death occurs in his own village. The third is like a
> man who does not awaken this mind until death occurs among
> his own family. And the fourth horse is like a man who awakens
> this mind only when his own death is imminent."*

In this analogy, the fact of death is first experienced as the death of someone distant from us, then the death of a close friend or family member, and finally by the fact of our own death. But just how closely do we relate to birth and death? Even at this moment, one of our monks is in the hospital and the doctor says there is no hope for recovery. All of us are experiencing it as something happening not to someone in a place far away but to someone closely related to us. What can we do about it? What can *I* really do with his life? With his sickness? And with his death?

We can look at our lives from the perspectives of these four kinds of horses. This whip has really hit *me*. And being whipped, I reflect upon myself and ask what is the best that I can do for our dying monk at this moment. How can we appreciate this life of birth, old age, sickness, and death? It is not just a matter of being in the hospital. What is the

* *Ibid.,* p. 113.

difference between right here now and there in the hospital? In a way, it is different. But if we see the wholeness of this life, then it is the same.

Dogen Zenji quotes from the *Mahaparinirvana Sutra:*

> The Buddha once said, there are four ways to control a horse. The first is to strike the horse's hair; the second, its skin; the third, its flesh; and the fourth, its bones. A rider's intentions are revealed to the horse by the location of the strike. Similarly, the Buddha used four ways to lead sentient beings to the Way. The first is to expound the law of birth. This is similar to a horse that finds the correct path as a result of having his hair struck by his rider. The second is to also expound the law of old age. This is like a horse that does the same after being struck on the skin. The third is to further expound the law of sickness. This equates with striking the horse's flesh. And the fourth is to include death in the explanation. This is like striking the horse's bones. A rider, however, is not always successful in leading a horse onto the right path. Shakyamuni, on the other hand, never fails to lead sentients to the Way. Thus he is known as the Great Controller of Man.*

Controller of Man, or the "person who has a good command of herself or himself," is one of the Buddha's ten nicknames. And what is the horse? The horse could be seen as the person who is trained to have good command of the self. What did the non-Buddhist see? What do we see? The horses run according to their sensitivity to the whip. How sensitive are we to illness, old age, and death as the very fact of reality?

We are living this life of impermanence, all experiencing it this very moment. How sharply are we sensing it? And if we do not feel it deep within our own bones, we are not the horse who runs at the shadow of the whip. Impermanence is the reality of change, the reality that is birth and death, rise and fall, creation and extinction. How are we truly appreciating this very moment, which may be the only moment we are living? If we do not see this, we do not understand impermanence.

* *Ibid.*, p. 113–14.

Let me read the last part:

> The receptive person realizes the Way merely on hearing the teaching on the law of birth. Others do not do so until old age has also been explained, and still others not until sickness and death have consecutively been added to the teaching. In a similar way, the three latter methods of controlling a horse occur only after the first has transpired. The latter three teachings of Shakyamuni—old age, sickness, and death—exist only as a result of the occurrence of the former on birth. It was Shakyamuni himself who initially proclaimed the law of birth, old age, sickness, and death. He did so not to break man's unity with these, nor to establish them as a standard of the Way. Rather, he used them as a means to lead sentient beings to the Way, a task in which he never fails.*

Dogen Zenji is saying that by talking about this life as old age, sickness, and death, we allow sentient beings to obtain the dharma of the unsurpassable Way. Shakyamuni Buddha talks about birth, sickness, old age, and death "to lead sentient beings to the Way, a task in which he never fails." Who is the person who never fails? Is it Shakyamuni Buddha or is it someone else who leads all sentient beings to the unsurpassable Way? How do *you* obtain this supreme wisdom?

Impermanence is always the plain, simple reality of our life, which is no other than the supreme Way itself. Those who see life in such a way run upon seeing the shadow of the whip. And when we see that the supreme Way is no other than our daily life, we must take good care of it. The best way to take care of it is to simply live the life of no division between birth or death, between this or that.

So what is life? What is sickness? Who is getting old? Who is dying? What are these different perspectives teaching us? It is not a matter of four kinds or two kinds of perspectives as such. Each one of us has a different life and yet the same life—the life of birth, illness, old age, and death. How do we best live this life of the supreme Way?

* Ibid., p. 114–115.

THE SEVEN WISE SISTERS

THE SEVEN WISE SISTERS is a rather unusual koan from Dogen Zenji's *Eihei Koroku,* his collection of 301 cases.

In India there was a very wealthy family of seven sisters who gathered together for a party every weekend. During a gathering, one of the sisters suggested, "Instead of having a party, let's go to the crematorium. I feel that if we go there, something good will happen." So they went to the crematorium and found corpses. Seeing the dead people, one of the sisters cried out, "All these corpses, where did the persons go?" Upon hearing this, all seven sisters simultaneously attained enlightenment.

The Hindu god Indra witnessed this. Impressed, he descended to talk to the sisters. "This is marvelous," he said, "I want to give you all a reward and will give anything you ask for." The sisters discussed what they wanted. "Do we want jewelry? No! We already have too many jewels. Money? We don't particularly care about it. Clothes? We have enough." Finally, they came up with three wishes and said to Indra, "We appreciate your offer, and have decided upon three things. First, we would like a rootless tree; second, a piece of land where there is no yin and yang; and third, a valley in which there is no echo." Indra said, "These are difficult things to give. Shakyamuni Buddha lives in your country. He will be able to grant your three wishes."

What are these three wishes? First, the sisters wish for a rootless tree. What is the rootless tree? Dogen Zenji says that the rootless tree is the "oak tree in the garden." That is a line from the famous Case 37 in the *Gateless Gate.* The monk asks Master Joshu, "What is the meaning of Bodhidharma's coming from the West?" In other words, what is the most important teaching of the Buddha? Master Joshu replies, "The oak tree in the garden." Dogen Zenji points to that oak tree in the garden as the rootless tree. The very state of enlightened life itself is now expressed as this rootless tree. How is this rootless tree your life?

The enlightened life is not fixed but free, unattached to any one thing. And yet, each of us is fixed or conditioned in certain ways. For instance, we have the condition of being human, of being a man or a woman, of having a family or being alone. We have certain knowledge giving rise to all sorts of ideas. All kinds of conditions and conditioning are like roots by which we survive. Is there anything wrong with this? Is there anything wrong with being attached to it? Our lives definitely have certain conditions. How is this so-called conditioned life the life of the rootless tree, the enlightened life?

Impermanence is among the Buddha's most fundamental teachings. How is impermanence generally understood? Instead of seeing how everything is constantly changing, we often think that there is something that does not change. Of course, we recognize certain change when it is noticeable, such as when a woman gives birth, when you move to a new home, or when someone leaves you. But are we aware of constant change or true impermanence? No, and consequently we live in a self-centered way. This self-centeredness is not necessarily derogatory of others. We are using self-centeredness here to mean that we create distinctions or certain boundaries where there are none. In one way or another, we are all self-centered. It is obvious that because of this conditioning, we invite problems. It happens because of *me*.

Who is *me*? In a way, all of us know *me*. And in a way, we do not know. We talk about big Self and small self. Is there truly something that is a big Self or a small self? If there is a big Self, can you show me how big it is? Whatever you understand as the small self, can you show me how small it is? How much difference is there between big Self and small self? I know you cannot show this to me. Why not? Because it is sizeless to begin with. This rootless tree is sizeless, constantly changing and unlimited by conditions. This is our life, do you see?

"The oak tree in the garden." The tree in the yard that the monk sees as an object is not at all an object for Master Joshu. There is no separation between the tree and himself. In fact, most of the time that is how we live. Even when we are not conscious of driving, when we come to a corner we stop, look, then turn and go on. The driver, car, street, signs, and signals *as they are* are all very clear, and yet no division comes up into the conscious mind. Amidst all relative conditions, we are freely driving. That is the rootless tree.

We can also look at the rootless tree a little differently. Let us say, for instance, that you do not understand what this rootless tree is. What is a tree with roots? Do you have a solid root by which your life is firmly grounded? We talk about body and mind in all kinds of ways: physical, emotional, psychological, mental, spiritual. What is the root of all these? Where is it? Is this body and mind solid and firm, stable and well functioning, sucking up enough nutrition from whatever ground on which it grows? On the other hand, if you do not see the solid ground, where could the root be? As a metaphor for your life, does this tree have a root or not? If you say yes, how and where does it grow? If no, why not? If your life has no root, how can you survive? Is having a root real or is not having a root real? Is your life real or is your life unreal? That is a silly question, isn't it? But, in fact, it is a truly fascinating question.

Regarding this rootless tree, Dogen Zenji says further, "If they don't understand the oak tree in the garden, I will hold up my staff and say, 'This staff is it!' " This is his second comment on the rootless tree. The oak tree in the garden and this staff in his hand. How do you appreciate it? "If you don't understand," he says, "this staff is it!" What does the staff stand for? The life of each of us is nothing but this staff, the oak tree, the rootless tree.

The seven sisters' second wish is a "piece of land where there is no yin and yang." Of course, yin and yang refers to opposites, duality. Dogen Zenji says, "This crematorium itself is that land where there is no yin and yang." In this instance, the crematorium is where the story occurs. The sisters ask, "The corpse is here, but where did the person go?" Anywhere, everywhere is nothing but this land where there is no yin and yang. Here, now! When there is death, there is nothing but death. When there is life, there is nothing but life. Dogen Zenji says further, "If they don't understand, I'll tell them that it is the 'Dharma-dhatu in all the ten directions.' "

The land where there is no yin and yang is the land upon which we stand right here, now. Even when our life seems fine, we have a problem when we see everything as opposites, as good or bad, right or wrong. What is good, what is bad? For instance, each tree is different. Some trees are big, some are small; some are crooked, some straight. Is there anything wrong with this? Being crooked, it is just crooked. Being straight, it is just straight. Some of us may think crooked is better than straight, or that a crooked tree should be straight. According to how we think about these opposites, problems arise.

Who creates these opposites? You might say that we do. But when we search for the answer, it is always *I* do. You cannot say *we*. What you may think of as good is not necessarily good to me or to someone else. I might compromise with you; I might understand or not understand. So when you say something is good, realize that it is what *you* think of as good. This is always the case. What happens if we do not have this *I*? As a matter of fact, then everything is okay.

The sisters' third wish is for the valley that has no echo. Here Dogen Zenji's comments are more direct. "Regarding this, I would call the seven sisters. If they respond, I will say immediately, 'I have just given you the valley.' And if they don't respond, I will say, 'Indeed, there is no echo.' " Regardless of whether you respond or not, right here you have this valley that has no echo. Fundamentally, our life is this unechoing valley. Our life itself is a synonym for the very best echoless valley. Isn't it marvelous?

In his *Song of Meditation,* Hakuin Zenji says, "All sentient beings are intrinsically buddhas." We are all right to begin with. So when called, just answer. If you cannot answer, that, too, is okay. Regardless of whether you answer or not, you are this fundamentally, originally enlightened ground. We practice on this ground of original enlightenment because that is our life. We do not need to look for anything else because everything is already right here. This life itself, *your* life itself, is the valley that has no echo. When you look for something else, you are putting another head on top of your own.

How do we appreciate the life that we have? Unfortunately, we often experience this life as if it were a roller coaster, spinning around in the six realms. Sometimes you feel marvelous. The next day, you hit bottom. You go from heaven to hell and all kinds of spheres in between from day to day, maybe even in one day. What are you doing with this life? You ask, "Am I really the same as the buddhas?" Many of you respond, "Hardly." So what will you do?

This is a very common dilemma. That is why if we just rely on one perspective, such as "We are all okay, be just as you are," we fall into a trap. It sounds good, but unfortunately, not all of us can live like that. Something is not quite right. We must examine who we are and truly see what this life is, what is the very nature of existence. This is a very natural inquiry. The important point is to have the understanding that is expressed in the seven sisters' three wishes.

So how do we practice in accordance with the insight of the seven wise sisters? Just sitting is fine. Polishing your insight with koans is also fine. Each of you must find the way in which you can comfortably practice. You are always at the very center. You are already in the Way. The realization of koan is your life! Each of us as we are is the realization of koan. And living our life is the practice of koan.

How can we appreciate our life as the rootless tree, as the land where there is no yin and yang, and as the valley with no echo? How are these three wishes the life of each of us? The important point is this life! Each of us is the treasure. How do we best take care of it? And taking care of this life is the best treasure we can have, isn't it?

Live the Life of Impermanence

DURING THE THIRTEENTH CENTURY Dogen Zenji gave a talk to his followers called "The Thirty-seven Conditions Favorable to Enlightenment." These thirty-seven conditions are very old principles relating to practice. They are the very best incomparable wisdom for living. One of these wisdoms is impermanence. How do we live fully a life of impermanence?

My mother died recently at the age of ninety, and her body was so small and light. I notice that even my own body, being over sixty years old, has begun to shrink. It happens. And that coldness of death. As a fact, I think ice is much colder than a human corpse. The coldness that comes with death is something very, very special. I am sure some of you have experienced it, and especially at such a moment, you felt a sense of impermanence or change. And perhaps you asked, "What is this life?" Suddenly we know how fleeting and perhaps even how insignificant our human life is.

"What's left behind?" we ask. Practically nothing is left, except maybe remains. And if we think something is left, what would it be? I do not mean to exaggerate, but I often have the feeling that my mother left everything. I sense this because I cannot discriminate what and how much she left. Furthermore, I sense to some degree that all I have is what has been left by her. Again I ask, "Just what do I have?" I do not know, but definitely something is there. This sense of impermanence can inspire us to confront our life.

When I myself think of impermanence, what comes up again is the *Abhidharma*'s teaching on how rapidly change is always taking place. We commonly consider ourselves to be living and then dying after fifty, seventy, or ninety years. But as I mention quite often, in a twenty-four-hour period alone we are being born and dying 6,500,000,000 times. It is so fast we cannot notice it. What is the nature of impermanence?

Let us appreciate together what Dogen Zenji teaches about this.

> First of all, there are the four types of meditation that eliminate false views: (1) contemplating the impurity of the body, (2) contemplating that perception leads to suffering, (3) contemplating the impermanence of mind, and (4) contemplating no-self [all things are devoid of self].*

What do we usually like to contemplate? We like to contemplate the beauty of one's physical body because that is what is usually promoted in our society. Instead, when we contemplate impermanence, we are contemplating the impurity of the body. So one might imagine a beautiful man or woman, and when this person dies, what happens to the

* Translation based on Nishiyama, vol. 2, p. 72.

beautiful body? It deteriorates. This change helps us realize the impermanence of life; we realize how transient life is, how such a beautiful,
attractive body changes into that which no one can even bear to see.
Our attachment to the body lessens. This resembles the original practice
of the old Buddhist monks who meditated in charnel grounds.

However, Dogen Zenji talks about this contemplation in a totally
different way. Let me read another passage about the contemplation of
impermanence:

> Concerning the "contemplation that the mind is impermanent,"
> Sokei (the sixth patriarch, Eno) the ancient buddha said, "Im-
> permanence is the Buddha nature." Great master Yoka Shingaku
> said, "All things are impermanent, everything is empty, this is
> the Tathagata's Great and Perfect Enlightenment." Contempla-
> tion of the mind's impermanence is the Tathagata's Great and
> Perfect Enlightenment. If the mind does not contemplate this,
> it falls into subjectivity. If there is mind, there must also be this
> contemplation.
>
> The actualization of supreme and total enlightenment is the
> impermanence and the contemplation of the mind. Mind is not
> necessarily permanent, nor is it separated from various pluralis-
> tic forms; even walls, tiles, stones, and large and small rocks are
> mind.*

This passage reminds me of the koan of Joshu's dog: A monk asks
Joshu, "Does a dog have Buddha nature or not?" Joshu said, "No."
According to the *Record of Joshu,* Joshu first says, "Yes." And the monk
asks, "If a dog has Buddha nature, how come he has the dirty skin of a
dog?" We think in a similar way, don't we? We think that Buddha nature
is something pure and genuine, which cannot be at all compared to
what we are, to whatever we have inside of this bag of skin. But this
impermanence itself *is* the Buddha nature.

* Ibid.

And what is this so-called mind? The mind is impermanent and that impermanence is the Buddha nature—the true nature, the unsurpassable Way. Contemplate this mind as impermanence which is the very life of the Buddha. Furthermore, that mind of impermanence and all its different manifestations are all together Buddha nature. This means not only us but everything: walls, tiles, mountains and rivers, shit stick, trash, literally everything. In other words, each of us and everything in this world are nothing but Buddha nature. And Buddha nature is nothing but the great, perfect enlightenment of Tathagata Buddha.

Dogen Zenji talks about contemplation, mind, and impermanence as one thing. This is a very important point. We usually separate these into three things. We say, "My mind contemplates impermanence," don't we? Dogen Zenji says these three are one. We live our life as impermanence, as the mind, as our zazen. Dogen says they're all one, everything is here.

So, for instance, when we look at life in this way, what is purity? What is impurity? What is delusion? What is enlightenment? If we make any distinction between Buddha nature or the Way itself and how we are actually living, then we are caught in the struggle between subject and object. However our life is, it is not excluded from that Buddha nature. Can we appreciate our life altogether as the life of the Buddha, regardless of the conditions in which we live?

Dogen Zenji says:

> Contemplation that all things are devoid of self is that long things are long, short things are short, in themselves. Realization and actualization exist, and therefore, there is no self.*

What does this mean? Long is long, short is short, a so-called pair of opposites. Actually, our life also appears to be made of opposites: suffering and joy, enlightened and deluded, good and bad, all kinds of dualities. Dogen Zenji says that these are all devoid of self. "Devoid of self" means "no fixed thing, no finite thing." If that is the case, what is there? How do we perceive this self?

* Ibid.

Our life comes about through causations, direct and indirect causations, and appears as conditions that are constantly changing. Having this body and mind is always the result of many, many causes, *all constantly changing*. When we really see this fact, right there is freedom. Such a life is itself no-self. Right here, all of us, each appearing distinctly different, are ourselves no-self, not fixed. We are constantly changing. In other words, we are totally free, liberated. If we could really see this, our life would be quite all right.

When we chant the *Heart Sutra* in Japanese, we chant *Kanjizai*. In the English version, Kanjizai, the "one who rests in the Self," is translated as Kanzeon, the "one who contemplates on the sounds of the world." Kanzeon appears as all the creatures he or she is contemplating, all the sounds he or she hears, and expounds the dharma as each and every one of them. So Buddha nature is a dog or you or me. When we say the dog has Buddha nature, we mean the dog *is* Buddha nature.

At the same time, being devoid of self, we appear to be simply what we are. Dogen Zenji repeats this over and over. Sentient beings are not Buddha nature because sentient beings are sentient beings, long is long, short is short. Dogen Zenji says, "All dharmas are no dharmas. That's the way to contemplate this mind devoid of self. If we grasp this, we can attain freedom from perplexity and doubt." You should know that everything is the activity of your life. This activity is all together the activity of Buddha nature, devoid of self, the activity of yourself as you are in each moment. This is what Dogen Zenji is expounding when he comments on whether a dog has Buddha nature or not.

Let me read a passage from the *Gakudo Yojinshu* in which Dogen Zenji comments on Joshu's dog:

> A monk asked Joshu, "Does a dog have Buddha nature or not?" Joshu replied, "*Mu* [non-being, negation]." Beyond this word *mu*, can you measure anything or grasp anything? There is entirely nothing to hold on to. Please try releasing your hold, and releasing your hold observe, what is body and mind? What is conduct? What is birth and death? What is Buddha dharma?

What are the laws of the world? What in the end are mountains, rivers, earth, human beings, animals, and houses?

What Dogen Zenji is talking about is clear, isn't it? It does not matter whether we think we have it or do not have it. The point is: what is it? The Sixth Patriarch illustrates this point in such a clear way: "Before you think good or evil, who are you?" Good and bad are just a pair of opposites. What is this body and mind all about? Instead of thinking *have* or *have not,* think about what you *are.*

Let me read what Dogen Zenji says in the very last paragraph of *The Thirty-seven Conditions Favorable to Enlightenment*:

> These thirty-seven conditions favorable to enlightenment are the enlightened eyes, the nostrils, the skin, flesh, bones, marrow, hands, feet, and face of the buddhas and patriarchs. Moreover, enlightenment is the actualization of 1,369 (37 × 37) conditions. Practice zazen continually, and drop off body and mind.*

That is to say, each condition contains all other conditions. This means that there are innumerable conditions. Again, this is the life of each of us, moment after moment. Being impermanent, being devoid of self, life goes in this way, moment after moment, six-and-a-half billion times a day; this is what is happening.

Dogen Zenji says, "Realize this and you will be liberated, you will realize the unsurpassable Way, the life of the Buddha, the real wisdom." The very ancient teaching is this vivid dynamic life of the buddhas and ancestors, which is no other than the life of each of us.

* Ibid.

DIVERSITY AND THE "RIGHT WAY"

I HEAR FROM MANY OF YOU how hard it is to have faith in the fact that we are the Way ourselves. Our so-called ordinary life is the way of difficulties and troubles. So what makes everyday life the way of the buddhas and ancestors? Do we live as human beings or as hungry ghosts in hell? Who among you can accept your life *as is* as the Way of the buddhas and ancestors?

Our senses perceive external phenomena through the six consciousnesses of eye, ear, nose, tongue, body, and mind. The seventh consciousness is the ego-conscious awareness, the consciousness that perceives life from our own ego-centered point of view. The eighth is the storage consciousness, which perceives all experience from beginningless time to the future, and the ninth consciousness is the so-called universal consciousness.

So how do we perceive this ordinary life?

Let us look at the five senses of eye, ear, nose, tongue, and body, which we use to perceive external objects. Even in the first stage of perception, are you perceiving the external world *as is* or as it comes through your five senses? There are all kinds of sounds, sights, sensations, and feelings. How are you perceiving them? And how does the sixth consciousness, the mind, function? For example, when all of us are listening to the same song at the same time, are we hearing the same thing? Some of you are annoyed by it, some are enjoying it, maybe some just notice the singing, and some are hardly paying any attention. Even at the earliest stage, we are already not perceiving things in the same way. We are already noticing and reacting to certain things differently according to our experiences, both direct and indirect. So already at the first stages there are big differences in the way we perceive things.

I like the word *diversity* because it captures all these differences. How are you reacting to this diversity with your discriminative mind? No two persons react in the same way. Every reaction is different. Our discriminative consciousness, the consciousness of the ego, involves literally billions of differences. The more sensitive you are, the larger the differences seem. Each of us has different experiences based on our varying cultural, religious, and racial backgrounds. Such a diversity! All these experiences are stored in the storage consciousness. These experiences are not only those that take place after we are born but also those from beginningless lives that we have all gone through.

We have only been human beings some fourteen million years. Our past lives in one way or another have been influencing this life. How much are we truly aware of these things? When we talk about our everyday life, our ordinary life, what kind of life are we talking about? We may think that our way is ordinary, but each of us is looking at it in an *extra*ordinary way, with biases based on our own experiences. How can we understand this everyday, ordinary life? How much can we say that the way *I* perceive is the right way?

Dogen Zenji tells us to forget ourselves. Are we instead reinforcing ourselves by the way we think and believe? Are our perceptions trustworthy? If something disturbs you and you express your anxiety about life, are you trusting your life as the Way itself, as the dharma itself? Your life is the same as the life of the buddhas and ancestors. Do you truly believe that? And believing in this way, can you really forget yourself? If you cannot forget yourself, what you are believing in is not the Buddha Way but something of yours that is troublesome.

How can we deal with this difficulty of our undivided life, our life as the Way, being chopped up into all these differences? All of us, as we are, are everything; we should not miss this point. When we realize it, then all this diversity—including these dichotomies of good and bad, right and wrong, male and female, night and day, life and death, whatever—is nothing other than the undivided Way manifesting as our ordinary life. Let the so-called body and mind go, unconfined by one's own thoughts. Our perceptions confine us, so how to be free? How to let ourselves function *as is?*

This undivided life of the buddhas and ancestors is manifesting as difference, as diversity. Please focus on how to appreciate this undivided and diverse life meaningfully and how to contribute in some way to decreasing the pain around us. Let us have more and more mutual respect and appreciation for each other, forgetting our own confinement in this unconfined life. I more than believe that you are the dharma yourself, that everyone and everything is the dharma itself. Please take good care of it.

THUSNESS

Great master Kokaku of Mount Ungan was the rightful heir of Tozan. He was the thirty-ninth dharma descendent of Shakyamuni Buddha and the rightful ancestor in the Tozan tradition. One day he addressed the assembly, saying: If one wants to attain the essence of thusness, one must become a person of thusness. But one is already a person of thusness, so why should one be anxious about the essence of thusness!*

—*Eihei Dogen,*
SHOBOGENZO IMMO

"THE ESSENCE OF THUSNESS" is enlightenment. Dogen Zenji says, "It is said that to think of attaining the essence of thusness is already to be a person of thusness. But one is already a person of thusness, so why should one be anxious about the essence of thusness." Which is to say that the as-it-is-ness is supreme enlightenment, and that is what we call thusness.

Thusness is no other than this very body and mind. How do you appreciate this? Dogen Zenji first expresses thusness in Chinese and then in Japanese. When we examine this line in Chinese, it means to want or to wish for enlightenment: "If one wants to attain the essence

* Hee Jin Kim, trans., "Flowers of Emptiness: Selections from Dogen's Shobogenzo," in *Studies in Asian Thought and Religion*, vol. 2. (Lewiston, NY: Edwin Mellen Press, 1985), 201.

of thusness, one must become a person of thusness." But Dogen Zenji rephrases it in Japanese in the following way: "To think of attaining the essence of thusness is already to be the person of thusness." Dogen Zenji says you are already thusness.

The *Nirvana Sutra* says that all beings have Tathagata Buddha's wisdom and virtue. How do we manifest or reveal ourselves as having the same wisdom as Tathagata Buddha, or reveal ourselves as the person of thusness? This is always the key to our practice. Whether your practice is shikantaza, koans, breathing, or something else, how do you understand this poem? Having the life we are living, we are already the person of thusness, the unsurpassable Way. Are we truly living as such a person?

> The nature of this supreme enlightenment is such that even the universe in all the ten directions is but a small portion of the supreme enlightenment. And the supreme enlightenment is still further beyond the entire universe. We are also various furnishings in the universe in all the ten directions. How do we know such is the case? The answer is, we know that such is the case because our bodies and minds manifest themselves in the entire universe and they are all selfless.*

"They are all selfless." In other words, with *I* and without *I*, including both relative and absolute. These ten directions, the entire world, are nothing but the body and mind of the person of thusness. The entire universe is nothing but each and every one of us. And at the same time, such a person is selfless. And being selfless, the person is able to manifest body and mind as the ten directions, as the entire universe.

There is the expression, the world in the ten directions is nothing but the illumination of one's self. So how to be this selfless person? We are already this person. What is preventing us from realizing it?

> Our bodies are not really ours. Life passes with time, never stopping for a moment. Where did our ruddy faces disappear

* Ibid, 201.

to? Although we look for them, their traces are nowhere. As we observe carefully, there are many things of the past we can no longer find. Neither do our sincere minds ever stand still; they go and come at every turn. Even though we have the mind of sincerity, it is not something sluggish surrounding the self. Within this context, there are people who arouse the mind all of a sudden; once the mind is aroused, they discard things they have hitherto indulged in; they desire to hear what they have not yet heard and seek to verify what they have not yet verified. All this has nothing to do with their personal efforts. We must know that this is so because they are persons of thusness. How do we know they are persons of thusness? We know they are persons of thusness because they think of attaining the essence of thusness.*

Dogen Zenji is talking about all of us. This passage makes me appreciate so very much all of you who are practicing. You know there is something that you must clarify, and yet your effort is not your effort. Whose effort is it? It is the effort of the person of thusness. Who is this person? Dogen Zenji says that even the hardship, anxiety, or whatever such a person experiences is also the essence of thusness. This is very true.

We say the true dharma eye looks for the true dharma eye. The true dharma eye comes to do zazen to *be* the true dharma eye, or manifest as such a person. In other words, you yourself as the true dharma eye manifests wherever you are as the true dharma eye.

We intrinsically have the countenance of the person of thusness, and so need not be anxious about the essence of thusness. Because anxiety is itself the essence of thusness, it is not anxiety. Moreover, we need not be startled by the essence of thusness being this way. Even if thusness appears startling and suspicious, it is thusness all the same: there is that thusness by which you

* Ibid, 201–202.

ought to be startled. It can't be measured by the measure of the Buddha, or the measure of the mind, any more than it can be measured by the measure of the dharma world, or the measure of the entire world. It is simply that "one is already a person of thusness; so why should one be anxious about the essence of thusness?"*

Isn't this wonderful? Your life cannot be measured by any restricted ruler. This reminds me of the koan by the Sixth Patriarch and Nangaku Ejo, which I have already referred to. "Who comes here as thus?" Nangaku spent eight years struggling with this koan. "Who am I?" is a fundamental inquiry. You know the answer intellectually. I am the whole world! I am this obvious fact: the person of thusness, the essence of thusness. This is my life, your life!

Nangaku said, "If you try to explain it, it doesn't hit the mark." What is the mark? Where is it? You yourself are the mark, and you yourself are the bow and arrow. You yourself are everything; that is the target. How can the target be hit? Is there any kind of special bow and arrow? This wisdom that Buddha manifests is innate in all of us. It is the life of each of us. How do each of you appreciate this thusness—the unsurpassable Way—as your life, as the life of the Buddha, as the wisdom of the Tathagata? It does not matter what you call it.

How do you take care of your anxiety, your frustration over this matter? "If one wants to attain the essence of thusness, one must become a person of thusness. But one is already a person of thusness, so why should one be anxious about the essence of thusness?"

* Ibid, 202.

On Becoming a Buddhist

WHEN YOU BECOME A BUDDHIST you receive the blood lineage chart. What is the most important implication of the blood lineage? The blood lineage is the lineage of Buddha, the Awakened One. Of course the lineage has been handed down from the patriarchs to us, and for this reason the teacher is crucially important. At the same time, all of you are as equal in importance as the teacher. We should not forget this.

This blood lineage, or the life of the Buddha, stems from Shakyamuni Buddha. Shakyamuni Buddha is not only a historical figure who lived some twenty-five hundred years ago, but also all the buddhas of the past, present, and future. All became Shakyamuni Buddha upon his attainment of Buddhahood. This Shakyamuni Buddha is called the eternal Shakyamuni Buddha.

Dogen Zenji writes that all the buddhas become Shakyamuni Buddha and that Shakyamuni Buddha becomes *this very mind is the Buddha*. This refers to the famous Case 30 of the *Gateless Gate*. A monk asks Master Baso, "What is Buddha?" Master Baso replies, "This very mind is Buddha." Penetrate this well. What is it? Who is it? Needless to say, all of you are that! This very mind is the Buddha; this very body is the Buddha!

When you realize Buddhahood, you yourself are identified with Shakyamuni Buddha. Then your life literally is the same as that of the whole universe. This is the insight of awakening. This is what Shakyamuni himself found out and declared: "I and the great earth, all beings, simultaneously attain the Way." This is Shakyamuni Buddha's prediction, his guarantee that all of us will eventually realize Buddhahood.

Upon his awakening Shakyamuni further declared, "How miraculous it is that all sentient beings have the same wisdom and virtue of Tathagata Buddha." To receive the precepts is to have the conviction that your life is simply the wisdom and virtue of Tathagata Buddha. Take care of yourself in this way. The ninth precaution in Dogen Zenji's *Ten Precautions on Learning the Way* (*Gakudo Yojin-Shu*) states that in order to truly take care of yourself, you should have faith that from the beginning, your life is one with the Way. This is a fact. There is no delusion and no confusion, no upside-down views, no increase and no decrease, and no mistakes. Dogen Zenji says raise this faith, clarify it, then practice in this way.

Our life as the Way itself is what gives value to our lineage. We are not just blindly believing in something; we raise such faith in the Way and make it work as our life. What is handed down to us? What is most precious? What is the vital, warm blood that runs through ourselves and through the lives of the buddhas and ancestors? What *is* the living essence of the lineage? Please take care of this most important matter.

When you become a Buddhist you go through the ceremony of receiving *jukai*. By Bodhidharma's definition, *jukai* means to become awakened to your own Buddha nature. *Ju* is "receiving," or "to transmit," and the implication of *kai* is "to awaken." So *jukai,* or receiving the *kai,* means to become awakened to your Buddha nature. We can say *jukai* literally means to receive the lineage, for the content of the lineage is your awakening to your own nature. Your own nature is called by different names, such as self nature, true nature, Buddha nature, no-nature, empty nature, mu. When you awaken to your own nature, right here is the liberation. Right here is the sphere in which the buddhas and ancestors reside, which is no other than the life of each of us. This is one way to describe the lineage.

On the lineage chart, the red bloodline goes in one continuous circle from your name back to Shakyamuni Buddha's name. The lineage is simply this one circle. When you receive jukai, your bloodline goes up into Shakyamuni Buddha. It is complete. At the conclusion of the jukai ceremony, we say: "When all beings receive the Buddha's kai, they all enter into the sphere of the Buddha." This sphere of the Buddha is the same as great enlightenment. "Indeed, we are the sons, daughters, children of the buddhas." The last verse of the ceremony verifies this one circle.

In one sense, receiving jukai is the ceremony of becoming a Buddhist, or at least becoming one who has faith in the Buddha Way. Who is the Buddha? Shakyamuni himself was Hindu. Being Hindu, he awakened and was called the Awakened One, or Buddha. So the word *buddha* means "awakened one" and was used even before Shakyamuni's enlightenment. In this sense, Buddhism is a general term. So we could say that being Christian or Jewish, you could also be Buddha. In this context, there is no contradiction in having another religious background, regardless of your commitment to practice the Buddha Way.

I appreciate many of you from different religious backgrounds, mostly Judeo-Christian, who are interested in practicing the Buddha Way. I have trouble finding the words to express my appreciation for your involvement. For example, being from Japan and growing up in a strong Buddhist environment, I would need lots of courage and determination to explore other religious practices. I express my appreciation and even admiration for all of you who have a commitment to Buddhism, to awakening.

From this angle we can also say it does not matter if you are Japanese, Chinese, black, brown, or white. Even the time does not matter. Anyone, anytime, can commit to accomplishing the awakened life. We do not need to label ourselves Buddhist. Just follow the enlightened Way, or the awakened Way. This is enough. In this sense, there is no conflict. You might even become a better Christian or Jew. So generally, Buddha's teaching is universal: one must truly be oneself as a human being, a man, a woman, whatever. This may be an extreme view, but basically Shakyamuni awakened, and as Buddha, the Awakened One, his concern was how to live this life in the best way possible.

ON LIFE AND DEATH

Firewood turns into ash, and does not turn into firewood again.
But do not suppose that the ash is after and the firewood is before.
We must realize that firewood is in the state of being firewood and has its
  before and after. Yet having this before and after, it is independent of
  them.
Ash is in the state of being ash and has its before and after.

Just as firewood does not become firewood again after it is ash, so after
one's death one does not return to life again.

Thus, that life does not become death is a confirmed teaching of the
buddha-dharma; for this reason, life is called the non-born.

That death does not become life is a confirmed teaching of the
buddha-dharma; therefore, death is called the non-extinguished.

Life is a period of itself.

Death is a period of itself.

For example, they are like winter and spring.

We do not think that winter becomes spring, nor do we say that spring
becomes summer.

—*Eihei Dogen,*
SHOBOGENZO GENJO KOAN

IN THIS PART OF THE *Genjo Koan,* Dogen Zenji makes a clear statement about life and death. He repeatedly talks about one's life as life
and death, as enlightenment and delusion, and as buddhas and beings.
This passage on life and death is all about one's practice, the practice of
the Buddha dharma. How do you appreciate your life as the Buddha
Way, which goes beyond all duality, beyond our assertions of this or
that? What is the action by which you give life to your true self? Dogen
Zenji's response is practice. What kind of practice? Practice as realization, as the Buddha Way.

Dogen Zenji teaches about practice as realization from beginning to
end. The most difficult part for us to see is the so-called no-self. What
does *no-self* mean? It is one of the crucial points relating to life and
death. "When the ten thousand dharmas are without self," he teaches,
then there is "no life and no death." Without self, whose death is it?
Without self, whose life are we talking about? Right now, here, who is
without self? Always right now, here, this *me* is without self. How do
you deal with it? Obviously you are dealing with it, adequately or inade-
quately, comfortably or uncomfortably, desperately, or however.

What is the turning point? We are the turning point ourselves, but
turning to what? This word *turn* has many implications in Japanese,

including "come back to." Come back to what? To the original self. The original self literally means *here*. Come back to here. From the very beginning, you have never gone anywhere. You have always been here. When you really turn back to here, all the ten thousand dharmas are without self. All ten thousand dharmas are Buddha dharma, the life of each of us. This is what we are appreciating.

We can be released from the confinement of the so-called *I*. We are enslaved by our understanding of *I*: *I* as a hungry ghost, *I* as this or that, or in its best sense, *I* as a human being. But what is the relationship between a human being and the Buddha Way? Is there anything more important than your life? Not your life as a hungry ghost, not even your life as a human being, but your life as the Buddha Way, as the very best unsurpassable Way. Dogen Zenji says that when a person is practicing that Way, he or she is called a buddha.

So who is dying? What kind of death are we talking about? When firewood burns, it becomes what we know as ash. Here Dogen Zenji is not saying that there is no death, nor that death does not exist. He is saying that life does not become death. Death has its own life. Life has its own life, and it has a before and after. We are born and living, there is a before and after, but life does not become death. Death does not become life, just as ash does not become firewood. You may wonder about the teachings of rebirth. We do not deny rebirth. According to karmic causations, whatever will happen, happens. But life still does not become death, death does not become life. It is unborn and undying. How do we understand this kind of life?

There are at least three different ways to understand life and death: in terms of division, in terms of change, and in terms of instances. Life and death in division is our usual understanding of being born. We live for ten, fifty, or sixty years, some of us for a short time, others longer, and then die. Life and death in terms of change is the life during which we realize some kind of enlightenment and are hence revitalized and born anew. But the most realistic life and death is the life and death of each instant. We are being born and dying 6,500,000,000 times every twenty-four hours.

The more I appreciate this, the more it becomes so real. I am very happy that I am having a new life every moment! I really mean it. Dogen Zenji writes in *Birth and Death* (*Shobogenzo Shoji*) that this life and death that we are encountering all the time is no other than the life of the Buddha. It is not only our life and death; all around us our relatives, close friends, and strangers are dying. We recently scattered someone's ashes on the mountainside. How do you practice a life that changes so much as the life of the Buddha?

There is a famous koan of Master Dogo and his student Zengen in the *Blue Cliff Record,* Case 55. Dogo was the elder brother of Ungan Donjo, Master Tozan's teacher. Even though he was the elder, Dogo did not become a monk until much later in life. He was a successful businessman and perhaps he thought that becoming a monk was ridiculous. However, his brother Ungan became a monk while young and studied for a long time with Master Hyakujo. Dogo was a brilliant man, and after becoming a monk, he advanced quickly and his understanding surpassed Ungan's. They were wonderful brothers.

The story is that one day Master Dogo and Zengen went to visit a family to perform a service for a dead family member. I do not know whether caskets were used or not in those days, but according to the story, Zengen hit the casket and asked Master Dogo, "Is this alive or dead?" The person was obviously dead. Being dead, is something alive or not? Even being a corpse, something is alive. Where? How? Is it alive or dead? Master Dogo replied, "I won't say, I won't say."

On their way back to the temple, Zengen was very serious. He asked again, "Is it alive or dead?" It is a serious question. All of us should be grabbed by this question. Am I really alive or not? As a human being, what kind of life is this? As the life of the Buddha, what is this? Zengen demanded of Dogo, "If you do not answer me, I am going to beat you up." He was that serious. Zengen was obviously not just asking whether the man had died or not. What was he really asking? Alive or dead?

It is the same thing that Dogen Zenji is talking about here. Since we will not die after death, it is called unborn and undying, or nonborn, nonextinguished. What does this mean? Your life is unborn, now, here. How to take care of it? Zengen actually beat up Master Dogo. And

Master Dogo said, "You'd better leave the temple. If others notice that you beat me up, they're going to beat you up." And Zengen left.

Now we are all laughing while I am telling this story, but I want you to take it seriously. Master Dogo and Zengen were so serious about resolving this issue of life and death. That is also why their realization is so clear. If you just listen to a talk and you feel that perhaps something is understood, it is still not convincing enough for you to confirm your life. You must experience yourself as the Buddha Way! That is why Zengen left. He had to experience the answer for himself.

Zengen went on a pilgrimage, and there are several other koans that record his practice after that. Finally he realized this grave matter of alive or dead. He was very appreciative of Master Dogo. Can I tell you just a little bit more? While on his pilgrimage, Zengen entered the dharma hall of a temple. The hall was very large. Upon entering, Zengen walked back and forth from the south end to the north end, from the north end to the south end, carrying a hoe. A monk saw him and asked, "What are you doing?" Can you imagine what Zengen responded? He said, "I am looking for the remains of my teacher." It is too much, isn't it?

Right now, however you are, *is* life. In Dogen Zenji's *Thorough Functioning* (*Shobogenzo Zenki*), he says life *is* manifestation. When it is manifested, it is the total realization of life and nothing else, and also it is the total manifestation of death and nothing else. What kind of life is Dogen Zenji talking about? It is not at all hard to understand. In one second, life and death is appearing and disappearing more than six thousand times. Dogen Zenji also says, "You have boundless dharma." In other words, in your life there are boundless, countless, innumerable dharmas. Life and death is one of these. How do you like it? You do not like it? I love it.

"There is death in the midst of life, and there is life in the midst of death." What kind of death, what kind of life is this?

BLOSSOMS OF NIRVANA

THERE IS A POEM about plum blossoms by Hata Zenji, the former chief abbot of Eiheiji monastery, which he gave to me when I once visited him.

White plum, one blossom,
two blossoms, three blossoms,
one thousand blossoms,
ten thousand blossoms.

What is this plum blossom? The plum blossom has five petals, which some say symbolizes the five schools of Chinese Zen. But it seems to me that these five schools are tiny compared with the real blossom of life. There is also the udumbara flower, which blooms once every three thousand years. Only some twenty-five-hundred years have passed since Shakyamuni Buddha appeared in the world, so what kind of flower is this? The lotus is also a primary blossom, as in the *Lotus Sutra*. What are these blossoms? The plum, the udumbara, and the lotus blossoms are all analogous to the life of each of us.

We appreciate this very life itself as the blossom of the Three Treasures when we observe Shakyamuni Buddha's Nirvana Day. What is nirvana? There are different definitions of nirvana, just as there are different kinds of blossoms. For example, we can look at nirvana as the extinction of passion, although you may not be satisfied with that definition. Passion is not necessarily something negative. Passion is a very important, positive energy. If we extinguish this energy, we are dead. So this view of nirvana is like a candle that burns and is finally extinguished.

What are some other kinds of nirvana? We say that when Shakyamuni Buddha attained realization, he entered nirvana. Being in nirvana, he still had to deal with the problems of the body and mind, such as illness, difficulties, and being disturbed in one way or another, just like you and me. Upon *parinirvana*, or his physical death, all these physical and mental difficulties were extinguished.

There are different implications to nirvana. Nirvana also refers to the genuineness of our own nature. In other words, our self nature is pure and genuine. What kind of blossom is this pure and genuine nature? Harada Sogaku Roshi, who was a brilliant scholar as well as a tough Zen master, wrote *The Eight Beliefs of Buddhism*. A more literal translation of the title would be "eight things that we can trust or have faith in."

The first belief is intrinsic Buddha nature. You are this nature now, at this very moment! What is intrinsic Buddha nature? Where is it? Buddha nature is not only no other than this very form, it is also everything. It is one blossom, a hundred blossoms, ten thousand blossoms. What is the difference between this body and mind and your true nature? Do you have any false nature? You, being as you are, are you false? Even to say true nature is funny. Nature has no true or false. What is it?

This leads us to the second belief, the misconception of the self or ego, *I*. Where does this *I* sneak in? One's understanding about oneself is somewhat deluded. How do these deluded thoughts occur? We recognize something that is not quite adequate, and we lose the vision of the true nature of life. The third belief is the continuity of life before and after death. If this life continues, how does it continue? And the fourth belief is the sureness of causation. This is relatively easy to understand, everything occurs by causation. We often speak of something as a coincidence or accident, but nothing happens without direct and indirect causes. The next belief is the existence of all buddhas. There exist those who have broken through the illusion of ego and have realized Buddha nature. The sixth belief is the mutual attraction between you and the buddhas. Without this mutual attraction, would we practice the Way? Would we seek nirvana? Not only are we seeking, but the Way itself is supporting us. All buddhas exist, how do you communicate with them? Where and how do they exist? Then, the seventh belief is that you and others are not two. Do you believe this? If you do, how sure are you about it? How can you confirm the fact that everything is dependent upon every other thing? And the eighth belief is that we are all in the process of becoming Buddha. All of us, without exception regardless of race, nationality, education and so forth, are becoming Buddha.

What is the relationship between the first belief of Buddha nature, that it is intrinsic, and the last belief, that we are all accomplishing the Buddha Way? Of course, it is not a matter of first and last, this is a continuous process, without beginning or end. If you do not see even one of these eight beliefs, you do not understand any of them. The reverse is also true. When you are sure of just one of these beliefs, you understand them all because all are connected. These are eight different aspects or perspectives of one fact. What is this fact?

Another definition of nirvana is no dwelling place. What is this dwelling nowhere? In other words, in this life we are not confined to any permanent or fixed state, so dwelling in no place is itself nirvana. Dogen Zenji urges us to take birth and death as nirvana itself. When you do this, you will dislike neither birth nor death, nor will you desire to attain nirvana. Thus, you are free from birth and death. This is the nirvana of no dwelling place, do you see? The *Platform Sutra* says that the Sixth Patriarch was enlightened upon hearing the line from the *Diamond Sutra*, "Dwelling in no place, raise the mind." In other words, being truly free and liberated, your life unfolds naturally, without obstructions, and that is nirvana.

So this Buddha nature is nirvana. This genuine nature is the blossom of your life. Dogen Zenji says: "Consider that nirvana is itself no other than our life." How do we experience this for ourselves? Such experience gives us indestructible strength; it gives us confidence, conviction, and peace. Our life is nothing but this blossom of nondwelling, nonattached nirvana. How can you confirm this for yourself?

UNKNOWN LIFE AND DEATH

SOONER OR LATER each of us dies. I want to share with you this inevitable fact. None of us knows how long we will live. We are not guaranteed tomorrow, not even today. We never know.

I was reading a story about a taxi driver who drank and argued with his wife all night long. Can you argue all night long? Maybe some of you have had that kind of experience. I myself have not, but I remember drinking all night long. Anyway, somehow the driver and his wife argued until morning, then he went to work at the Sapporo airport in Hokkaido, the northernmost island of Japan. Four men on a business trip arrived from Kyushu and asked the driver to take them to a town about a half hour away. The men asked the driver to wait while they conducted their business. After a while they returned and told the driver that they had time to do some sightseeing. The taxi driver drove to a lake, and after about an hour of sightseeing, the taxi plunged into the lake. The driver survived, but all four passengers were killed.

The author of the story asks us to consider how many people suffer when one person dies. He says maybe five hundred people. I do not know if five hundred is a large or a small number, but if that is the number to use, then in this instance two thousand people suffered. How do we think about these four passengers, or about anyone who has died? What are they doing now? Have they completely disappeared? Or is something remaining and continuing in some way? In fact, Dogen Zenji says, "After we die, what continues is the karma we created, both good and bad." What does this mean?

Life and death is a primary theme that we must clarify. We are all concerned about death in one way or another. What will happen after we die? This reminds me of a book by a medical doctor and professor at Tokyo University who died of cancer in 1962. I knew him because although he was a Christian, he sat with my teacher Koryu Roshi and even gave talks in the zendo. As a doctor, he was always dealing with someone else's sickness. But when he himself had cancer, he had to deal with his own illness; it was now his own issue. What kind of struggles did he go through? During that time he wrote a book about his understanding of what was going to happen after his death. He felt that life ends after death. Perhaps he reached that kind of conclusion because he was a scientist.

The author of the story about the taxi driver takes a different position. He says that we do not know what is going to happen after death. He does not take any position about extinction or continuation of some kind; rather, he says it is unknown. In other words, it cannot be known through our logical, intellectual speculation. I agree with this. What I myself have been seeing more and more is how little we know. How little we know! And when we make any assertion relating to what is going to happen after death, who can really reply with a definite, one hundred percent, for sure answer?

Before birth is another aspect. Before you were born, what was your life? Was it existing or not existing? Definitely it was not existing as the life that you are living right now, but as sure as all of us die in one way or another, sooner or later we also come from somewhere. Without our parents, our parents' parents, and our parents' parents' parents, we would not be here. If we come from somewhere before birth, are we going somewhere after death?

The Buddha talked about life and death as his major concern. In his first sermon on the Four Noble Truths, the first truth was that life is suffering. Being born is suffering, being ill is suffering, growing old is suffering, dying is suffering. Why are they all suffering? Buddha talks about *I*. He says that there is no such thing as this *I* that we hold on to. Instead, there is impermanence and no substantial self. At the same time, he tells us to take good care of this *I*. Make this *I* as the dharma, as the teaching, the torch that shines upon your life. How do we see these different aspects of life? And facing these sufferings of life, how do we detach from holding on? I think the major holding on, in one way or another, is to oneself, to this *I*.

I myself have faith in the fact that this life will not end when I die. This means I will die and I will not die. I believe that regardless of how true it is. And if people say that I am wrong, I accept it; it does not make any difference to me. This unborn, undying life, which has been continuing, is very important. We do not know exactly how it has been continuing, but we know for sure that without the unborn, undying life, our life would not be here. Isn't this so? So how do we appreciate this unknown part of our life?

We try to understand our life in our heads. This is a very drunken state, more drunk than the taxi driver. Why? Of course, the driver did an awful thing. He caused four people to die and made at least two thousand people suffer. But when we ourselves are not sober, when we ourselves are not aware of this unborn, undying life, we are also killing, do you see? Killing the life of what? We are killing the life of the buddhas and ancestors.

I appreciate the unknown energy or life force that is supporting us, making things happen and keeping our life going. Things that happen are not casual coincidences. How do we appreciate this flow of our life, regardless of whether it is pleasant, unpleasant, joyous, or painful? Our actions always have causes and effects. So in sharing our life together, let us be kind to each other and to ourselves as much as we can.

SHAKYAMUNI BUDDHA AND I ARE PRACTICING TOGETHER

THE CHINESE ZEN MASTER Gensha lived in the late Tang dynasty a little over twelve hundred years ago. One day while Gensha and his father were fishing, the father drowned. Gensha stopped being a fisherman and went to Master Seppo's monastery, where he ordained as a monk. At that time Gensha was already thirty years old, in those days a fairly advanced age for ordination and training.

Master Seppo was a very famous Zen master. It is said that fifteen hundred monks were practicing at his monastery. After two years, Gensha embarked on a pilgrimage to other monasteries. While walking, he stubbed his toe on a sharp rock. Gensha cried out, "Where does this pain come from?"

This body is empty, so where does pain come from? When we stub our toe, don't we usually shout, "This dumb rock!" or "I am so stupid!" What kind of awareness do we have? Yet in Gensha's case, he asked, "Where does this pain come from?" And at that instant, he attained realization.

Gensha immediately returned to Master Seppo. Seeing Gensha limping, Master Seppo asked, "Why aren't you on your pilgrimage?" Gensha replied, "Bodhidharma has never come from India, and the second patriarch has never gone to India. Bodhidharma and I are walking together hand in hand. Bodhidharma is no other than myself. I am the second patriarch, going nowhere. Being *here* is my life! Shakyamuni Buddha and I are sitting together, sharing life together, living together, breathing together, counting together, being drowsy together."

Now, we all know that Bodhidharma came from India and that his successor, the Second Patriarch (Taiso Eka) in China, never went to India. So what did Gensha mean?

Gensha became one of the best of Master Seppo's many successors, and yet he had a very difficult time in practice. He was determined to resolve his doubts, and his questioning was most important. Being in his thirties, Gensha had probably formed a certain understanding about life and was perhaps not so flexible. How did he empty himself? He was training in a huge monastery with fifteen hundred other monks. How much of a chance did he have to talk to Master Seppo? Perhaps they rarely spoke, and yet Gensha attained realization. How did this happen? How about the other hundreds of monks? And how about you?

You may be asking, "Will this happen to me? How can I confirm myself?" Gensha realized himself as Shakyamuni Buddha, as Bodhidharma, as the Second Patriarch. This is true for all of us. Regardless of whether we realize it or not, our life *is* the life of Shakyamuni Buddha. We are sharing that life together. Gensha realized this by not confining himself to the usual ways of thinking.

We are all on some kind of quest. We have some determination to know who we are or how to pursue our life in the best way. What is the difference between Gensha and ourselves? What creates the obstacles that keep us from seeing what Gensha saw? What creates the hindrances that prevent each of us from seeing himself or herself as the one who is constantly dancing, singing, and talking with Shakyamuni Buddha? All of us must see this for ourselves. No one can do it for us.

How do you confirm yourself as "Shakyamuni and I are practicing together, living together"? In order to experience this, you need to do something with your busy mind. By counting your breath you can trim off busy thoughts, rising like bubbles, one after another. Are you practicing with bubbles instead of with Shakyamuni Buddha? By counting your breaths in cycles of ten, all these numerous thoughts are reduced to ten. By following the breath, you reduce it to two, inhalation and exhalation. But it is not simply a matter of two, ten, or one hundred. Don't forget, breathing is life. By breathing genuinely in this way, you begin to live in this way. In what way? You appreciate intimately the life that you are living *in this very moment.*

When I was in college, I lived in a dormitory where I studied with Koryu Roshi. Koryu Roshi often said, "When you breathe in, breathe in the whole universe. When you breathe out, breath out the whole universe. Breathing in and out, in and out, eventually you even forget about who is breathing what." There is no inside, no outside; no this, no that. Everything is all together disappearing. So what is there? You can answer, "Nothing." When you truly sit, you can also say, "Everything."

When we understand Master Gensha's statement, all of our questions about practice will be resolved. Have trust in your life as the Way itself. Have trust in yourself as Shakyamuni Buddha himself. I want you to appreciate this. This is not a sophisticated teaching. Your life *is* "Shakyamuni Buddha and I are practicing together." Please have good trust in yourself.

GENJO KOAN
by Eihei Dogen

> *When all dharmas are buddha-dharma, there are*
> *enlightenment and delusion, practice, life and death,*
> *buddhas and creatures.*
> *When the ten thousand dharmas are without self,*
> *there are no delusion, no enlightenment, no*
> *buddhas, no creatures, no life and no death.*
> *The buddha way transcends being and non-being;*
> *therefore there are life and death, delusion and*
> *enlightenment, creatures and buddhas.*
> *Nevertheless, flowers fall with our attachment, and weeds*
> *spring up with our aversion.*

To carry the self forward and realize the ten thousand
dharmas is delusion.

That the ten thousand dharmas advance and realize
the self is enlightenment.

It is buddhas who enlighten delusion.

It is creatures who are deluded in enlightenment.

Further, there are those who attain enlightenment
above enlightenment; there are those who are
deluded within delusion.

When buddhas are truly buddhas, one need not be
aware of being buddha.

However, one is the realized buddha and further
advances in realizing buddha.

Seeing forms with the whole body and mind, hearing
sounds with the whole body and mind, one
understands them intimately.

Yet it is not like a mirror with reflections, nor like water
under the moon —

When one side is realized, the other side is dark.

To study the buddha way is to study the self.

To study the self is to forget the self.

To forget the self is to be enlightened by the ten
thousand dharmas.

To be enlightened by the ten thousand dharmas is to
free one's body and mind and those of others.

No trace of enlightenment remains, and this traceless
enlightenment is continued forever.

When one first seeks the truth, one separates oneself
far from its environs.

When one has already correctly transmitted the truth
to oneself, one is one's original self at that
moment.

When riding on a boat, if one watches the shore one
may assume that the shore is moving.

But watching the boat directly, one knows that it is the
  boat that moves.
If one examines the ten thousand dharmas with a
  deluded body and mind, one will suppose that
  one's mind and nature are permanent.
But if one practices intimately and returns to the true
  self, it will be clear that the ten thousand dharmas
  are without self.
Firewood turns into ash and does not turn into
  firewood again.
But do not suppose that the ash is after and the
  firewood is before.
We must realize that firewood is in the state of being
  firewood and has its before and after. Yet having
  this before and after, it is independent of them.
Ash is in the state of being ash and has its before and after.
Just as firewood does not become firewood again after
  it is ash, so after one's death one does not return to
  life again.
Thus, that life does not become death is a confirmed
  teaching of the buddha-dharma; for this reason,
  life is called the non-born.
That death does not become life is a confirmed
  teaching of the buddha-dharma; therefore, death
  is called the non-extinguished.
Life is a period of itself.
Death is a period of itself.
For example, they are like winter and spring.
We do not think that winter becomes spring, nor do we
  say that spring becomes summer.
Gaining enlightenment is like the moon reflecting in
  the water.
The moon does not get wet, nor is the water disturbed.
Although its light is extensive and great, the moon is
  reflected even in a puddle an inch across.

The whole moon and the whole sky are reflected in a
    dew-drop in the grass, in one drop of water.
Enlightenment does not disturb the person, just as the
    moon does not disturb the water.
A person does not hinder enlightenment, just as a dew-drop
    does not hinder the moon in the sky.
The depth of the drop is the height of the moon.
As for the duration of the reflection, you should
    examine the water's vastness or smallness,
And you should discern the brightness or dimness of
    the heavenly moon.
When the truth does not fill our body and mind, we
    think that we have enough.
When the truth fills our body and mind, we realize that
    something is missing.
For example, when we view the four directions from a
    boat on the ocean, where no land is in sight, we see
    only a circle and nothing else.
No other aspects are apparent.
However, this ocean is neither round nor square, and
    its qualities are infinite in variety. It is like a
    palace. It is like a jewel. It just seems circular as
    far as our eyes can reach at the time.
The ten thousand dharmas are likewise like this.
Although ordinary life and enlightened life assume
    many aspects, we only recognize and understand
    through practice what the penetrating power of
    our vision can reach.
In order to appreciate the ten thousand dharmas, we
    should know that although they may look round
    or square, the other qualities of oceans and
    mountains are infinite in variety; furthermore,
    other universes lie in all quarters.
It is so not only around ourselves but also right here,
    and in a single drop of water.

When a fish swims in the ocean, there is no limit to
the water, no matter how far it swims.
When a bird flies in the sky, there is no limit to the air,
no matter how far it flies.
However, no fish or bird has ever left its element since
the beginning.
When the need is large, it is used largely.
When the need is small, it is used in a small way.
Thus, no creature ever comes short of its own
completeness.
Wherever it stands, it does not fail to cover the ground.
If a bird leaves the air, it will die at once.
If a fish leaves the water, it will die at once.
Know, then, that water is life.
Know that air is life.
Life is the bird and life is the fish.
Beyond these, there are further implications and
ramifications.
In this way, there are practice and enlightenment,
mortality and immortality.
Now if a bird or a fish tries to reach the limit of its
element before moving in it, this bird or this fish
will not find its way or its place.
Attaining this place, one's daily life is the realization of
ultimate reality (genjokoan). Attaining this way,
one's daily life is the realization of ultimate reality
(genjokoan).
Since this place and this way are neither large nor
small, neither self nor other, neither existing
previously nor just arising now, they therefore
exist thus.
Thus, if one practices and realizes the buddha way,
when one gains one dharma, one penetrates one
dharma; when one encounters one action, one
practices one action.

Since the place is here and the way leads everywhere,
the reason the limits of the knowable are
unknowable is simply that our knowledge arises
with, and practices with, the absolute perfection of
the buddha-dharma.
Do not practice thinking that realization must become
the object of one's knowledge and vision and be
grasped conceptually.
Even though the attainment of realization is
immediately manifest, its intimate nature is not
necessarily realized. Some may realize it and some
may not.

Priest Pao-ch'e of Ma-Kushan was fanning himself. A monk approached and asked, "Sir, the nature of the wind is permanent, and there is no place it does not reach. Why, then, must you still fan yourself?" "Although you understand that the nature of wind is permanent," the master replied, "you do not understand the meaning of its reaching everywhere." "What is the meaning of its reaching everywhere?" asked the monk. The master just fanned himself. The monk bowed with deep respect. This is the enlightened experience of buddha-dharma and the vital way of its correct transmission. Those who say we should not use a fan because wind is permanent, and so we should know the existence of wind without using a fan, know neither permanency nor the nature of wind.

Because the nature of wind is eternally present, the wind of Buddhism actualizes the gold of the earth and ripens the cheese of the long river.

Written in mid-autumn of the first year of Tempuku Era (1233 C.E.) and given to my lay student Yo Koshu of Kyushu.

Printed with permission of Zen Center of Los Angeles. This is a revision by Taizan Maezumi and Francis Dojun Cook of the Chotan Aitken Roshi-Kazuaki Tanahashi translation in The Way of Everyday Life: Zen Master Dogen's Genjokoan with Commentary *by Hakuyu, Taizan Maezumi. Los Angeles, Center Publications, © 1978.*

Fukanzazengi
(Principles of Seated Meditation)
by Dogen Zenji
translated by Carl Bielefeldt

Fundamentally speaking, the basis of the way is perfectly pervasive; how could it be contingent on practice and verification? The vehicle of the ancestors is naturally unrestricted; why should we expend sustained effort? Surely the whole being is far beyond defilement; who could believe in a method to polish it? Never is it apart from this very place; what is the use of a pilgrimage to practice it? And yet, if a hair's breadth of distinction exists, the gap is like that between heaven and earth; once the slightest like or dislike arises, all is confused and the mind is lost.

Though you are proud of your understanding and replete with insight, getting hold of the wisdom that knows at a glance, though you attain the way and clarify the mind, giving rise to the spirit that assaults the heavens, you may loiter in the precincts of the entrance and still lack something of the vital path of liberation. Even in the case of the one of Jetavana, innately wise though he was, we can see the traces of his six years sitting erect; and in the case of the one of Shao-lin, though he succeeded to the mind seal, we still hear of the fame of his nine years facing the wall. When even the ancient sages were like this, how could men today dispense with pursuing [the way]? Therefore, stop the intellectual practice of investigating words and chasing after talk; study the backward step of turning the light and shining it back. Body and mind will drop away of themselves, and your original face will appear. If you want such a state, urgently work at such a state.

For studying Zen, one should have quiet quarters. Be moderate in food and drink. Cast aside all involvements and discontinue all affairs. Do not think of good or evil; do not deal with right or wrong. Halt the revolutions of mind, intellect, and consciousness; stop the calculations of thoughts, ideas, and perceptions. Do not intend to make a Buddha, much less be attached to sitting still.

In the place where you regularly sit, spread a thick mat and use a cushion on top of it. Sit in either the full cross-legged or half cross-legged position. For the full position, first place your right foot on your left thigh; then place your left foot on your right thigh. For the half position, simply rest your left foot on your right thigh.

Loosen your robe and belt, and arrange them properly. Next, place your right hand on your left foot, and your left hand on your right palm. Press the tips of your thumbs together. Then straighten your body and sit erect. Do not lean to the left or right, forward or backward.

Your ears should be in line with your shoulders, and your nose in line with your navel. Press your tongue against the front of your palate and close your lips and teeth. The eyes should always remain open. Breathe gently through the nose.

Once you have regulated your posture, take a breath and exhale fully. Swing to the left and right. Sitting fixedly, think of not thinking. How do you think of not thinking? Nonthinking. This is the essential art of zazen. Zazen is not the practice of dhyana: it is just the dharma gate of ease and joy. It is the practice and verification of ultimate bodhi. The koan realized, baskets and cages cannot get to it.

If you grasp the point of this [practice], you are like the dragon gaining the water or the tiger taking to the mountains. You should realize that when right thought is present, dullness and agitation are, from the start, struck aside.

When you arise from sitting, move slowly and arise calmly; do not be hasty or rough.

Considering the past, we see that transcending the profane and surpassing the holy, shedding [this body] while seated and fleeing [this life] while standing are totally subject to this power. Surely, then, to grasp the turning of the opportunity through a finger, a pole, a needle or a mallet, and to present the verification of the accord with a whisk, a fist, a staff or a shout—these are not to be understood through the discriminations of thinking; much less can they be known through the practice and verification of supernormal powers. They must represent conduct beyond sound and form; how could they fail to provide a standard before knowledge and understanding?

Therefore, it does not matter whether one is very smart or very stupid; there is no distinction between those of sharp and dull faculties. Single-minded exertion is itself pursuit of the way. Practice and verification are by nature undefiled. Advancement [to enlightenment] is just an everyday affair. In our world and the other quarters, from the Western Heaven to the Eastern Earth, all equally maintain the Buddha seal, while each enjoys its own style of teaching. They devote themselves only to sitting; they are obstructed by fixedness. Though they speak of ten thousand distinctions and a thousand differences, they only study Zen and pursue the way.

Why abandon the seat in your own home to wander in vain through the dusty regions of another land? If you make one false step, you miss what is right before you. Since you have already attained the functioning essence of a human body, do not pass your days in vain; when one takes care of the essential function of the way of the Buddha, who can carelessly enjoy the spark from a flint? Verily form and substance are like the dew on the grass, and the fortunes of life like the lightning flash: in an instant they are emptied, in a moment they are lost.

Eminent students [of the dharma], long accustomed to groping for the elephant, pray do not doubt the true dragon. Apply yourselves to the way that points directly at reality; honor the man who is through with learning and free from action. Accord with the bodhi of all the Buddhas; succeed to the samadhi of all the Patriarchs. If you act this way for a long time, you will be this way. Your treasure store will open of itself, and you will use it as you will.

Printed with permission from University of California Press.

Source: Carl Bielefeldt, *Dogen's Manuals of Zen Meditation*. (Berkeley: University of California Press, 1988), 175–187.

THE IDENTITY OF RELATIVE AND ABSOLUTE
by Sekito Kisen

The mind of the Great Sage of India
Is intimately conveyed west and east.
Among human beings are wise ones and fools;
In the Way, there is no teacher of north and south.
The subtle source is clear and bright,
The branching streams flow in the dark.
To be attached to things is primordial illusion,
To encounter the absolute is not yet enlightenment.
All spheres, every sense and field,
Intermingle even as they shine alone,
Interacting even as they merge
Yet keeping their places in expressions of their own.
Forms differ primarily in shape and character,
And sounds in harsh or soothing tones.
The dark makes all words one;
The brightness distinguishes good and bad phrases.
The four elements return to their true nature as a child to its mother.
Fire is hot, water is wet; wind moves and the earth is dense.
Eye and form, ear and sound,
Nose and smell, tongue and taste—the sweet and sour.
Each independent of the other like leaves that come from the same root;
And though leaves and root must go back to the Source,
Both root and leaves have their own uses.
Light is also darkness, but do not move with it as darkness.
Darkness is light; do not see it as light.
Light and darkness are not one, not two,
Like the foot before and the foot behind in walking.
Each thing has its own being, which is not different from its place and
    function.
The relative fits the absolute as a box and its lid.
The absolute meets the relative
Like two arrows meeting in midair.

Hearing this, simply perceive the Source!
Make no criterion: if you do not see the Way,
You do not see It even as you walk on It.
When you walk the Way, you draw no nearer, progress no farther.
Who fails to see This *is mountains and rivers away.*
Listen, those who would pierce this Subtle Matter,
Do not waste your time by night or day!

Printed with permission from the Zen Community of New York.

AVALOKITESHVARA. (Sanskrit). Bodhisattva or incarnation of compassion. In Japanese, Kanjizai, or "One who rests in the Self," or Kanzeon, "One who hears the sounds of the world."

BODHI. (Sanskrit) (lit. "awakened"). In Zen, bodhi is the wisdom of awakening to the true nature, or essential emptiness, of all things.

BODHI MIND. Mind in which an aspiration to enlightenment has been awakened.

BODHIDHARMA. Indian adept recognized as the founder and first patriarch of Zen in China in the early sixth century.

BODHISATTVA. (Sanskrit) (lit. "enlightenment being"). One who seeks enlightenment through the compassionate vow to liberate all beings. An ideal of Mahayana Buddhism.

BUDDHA NATURE. The intrinsic or essential nature of all sentient beings, whether realized or not, and of all things.

DHARMA. (Sanskrit). Things or phenomena; mental objects, the teachings of the Buddha; also Universal Law or Truth, Buddhist doctrines.

DHARMADHATU. (Sanskrit) (lit. "realm of dharma"). In Mahayana Buddhism, the true nature that permeates and encompasses all phenomena. Also the dharma realm of totality in which all phenomena arise and pass away.

DOGEN ZENJI. (1200–1253). Founder of Japanese Soto Zen school. Known formally as Eihei Dogen (Zenji) or Dogen Kigen. After studying for nine years under Rinzai teacher Myozen, Dogen undertook the difficult journey to China, studied with and became a dharma successor to Tendo Nyojo (T'ien-t'ung Ju-ching) in the Soto Zen lineage. In Japan, he established Eiheiji, the principal Soto training monastery, and wrote *Shobogenzo*, a philosophical explanation of Buddhism containing ninety-five chapters, generally considered to be one of the most profound and outstanding works of religious literature. Dogen Zenji emphasized the practice of shikantaza but did not discount the use of koans in Zen training.

DOKUSAN. (Japanese). Face-to-face encounter between Zen master and student in which the student's understanding is probed and stimulated. During dokusan, a student may consult with the master on any matter arising directly out of practice.

EIGHT AWARENESSES. According to *Mahaparinirvana Sutra*, the final teaching of Shakyamuni Buddha: having few desires, knowing how to be satisfied, enjoying serenity and tranquility, exerting meticulous effort, not forgetting [right] thought, practicing samadhi, cultivating wisdom, and avoiding idle talk.

EIGHTFOLD PATH. Fourth Noble Truth in which Shakyamuni Buddha taught the way to end suffering. The eightfold path consists of right (total, complete) understanding, thought, speech, action, livelihood, effort, mindfulness, and samadhi.

ENLIGHTENMENT. Realization of one's true nature. In Japanese, kensho.

FOUR NOBLE TRUTHS. Shakyamuni Buddha's earliest and most fundamental teachings concerning the nature of life and how to live it. (1) There is suffering (dukkha) in life; (2) suffering has a cause;

(3) there is a way to end the cause of suffering; (4) that way is the eightfold path.

THE GATELESS GATE. In Japanese, *Mumonkan*. Important collection of 48 koans compiled with commentary by 13th-century Chinese Zen Master Mumon Ekai (Wu-men Hui-k'ai). Begins with renowned koan "Mu."

GENJO-KOAN. (Japanese) (roughly "Everyday Life is Enlightenment"). Essay by Dogen Zenji written originally for a lay student and later contained in his work Shobogenzo. Genjo-koan also refers to everyday life koans, questions or situations that naturally arise in one's life that help bring one to realization.

JUKAI. (Japanese). The ceremony of receiving the bodhisattva precepts. Person receiving the precepts formally becomes a Buddhist and receives the Buddha's robe (rakusu), a lineage chart, and a dharma name.

KOAN. A text or question—traditionally taken from, but not limited to, Zen literature—assigned to a student by the teacher. The student must then demonstrate a clear grasp of the essence of the koan.

LOTUS SUTRA. (Sanskrit) (*Saddharmapundarikasutra*, "Sutra of the Lotus of the Good Dharma"). One of the most important sutras of Mahayana Buddhism, particularly in China and Japan. In the *Lotus Sutra*, the Buddha appears as a manifestation of true nature, with which everyone is fully endowed and can, therefore, awaken.

MAHAYANA. (Sanskrit) (lit. "great vehicle"). School of Buddhism that emphasizes that practice is not for oneself alone, but for the liberation of all beings.

NIRVANA. (Sanskrit) (lit. "extinction"). In Zen, a non-dualistic state beyond life and death. Also refers to a state of peace or bliss, which arises when one realizes the true nature of life and lives free from attachments.

RINZAI SCHOOL. One of the two most important schools of Japanese Zen, founded by Master Rinzai (d. 866 or 867). Rinzai Zen is characterized by its use of koan practice to attain realization of one's own nature.

SAMADHI. (Japanese). State of mind characterized by one-pointedness of attention. Also a non-dualistic state of awareness, characterized by putting all of one's self into each activity.

SELF-FULFILLED SAMADHI. (Japanese) (*Jijuyu zanmai*; roughly, "To receive yourself and use yourself freely"). State of total immersion in one's life so that everything encountered is encountered fully as the natural functioning of oneself.

SHIKANTAZA. (Japanese) (lit. "just-sitting," or "only sitting"). Practice of zazen itself without supportive devices such as breath counting or koans. Characterized by intense, non-discursive awareness; shikantaza is "zazen doing zazen for the sake of zazen."

SOTO SCHOOL. One of the two most important schools of Japanese Zen, founded by Masters Tozan Ryokai (Tung-shan Liang-chieh, 809– 869) and Sozan Honjaku (Ts'ao-shan Pen-chi, 840–901) and named by combining the first characters of their names. Introduced to Japan by Dogen Zenji. Soto Zen stresses "silent illumination Zen" without the use of koans and is characterized by the practice of shikantaza.

TATHAGATA. One of the ten titles of the Buddha, literally "the thus-come one" or "the thus-perfected one."

THE TEN DIRECTIONS. In Buddhist cosmology the ten directions include the four cardinal directions, the four intermediate directions, the zenith, and the nadir.

TENKEI DENSON ZENJI. (1648–1735). The great Soto Zen teacher and scholar who wrote the first commentaries on Dogen's *Shobogenzo*.

TEISHO. (Japanese). Formal presentation by a Zen master, usually on a koan or other Zen text. In strictest sense, a teisho is a living presentation of non-dualism and is thus distinguished from dharma talks, which are lectures on Buddhist topics.

THE THREE TREASURES. Three essential aspects of Buddhism: Buddha (the Awakened One), Dharma (the teachings of the Awakened One), and Sangha (community of those practicing Buddhism together).

VAIROCHANA BUDDHA. One of five transcendent buddhas identified as the embodiment of dharmakaya (unified existence beyond all duality). His mudra (hand position), used by many Zen practitioners during zazen, is that of supreme wisdom.

ZENDO. Place set aside for the practice of zazen.

ZENJI. Honorific title meaning "Zen teacher or master." Often re-
served for the abbots of Eiheiji and Sojiji, the main monasteries in
the Japanese Soto school. Maezumi Roshi also used it for esteemed
Zen ancestors.

BIBLIOGRAPHY

Cleary, Thomas, and J. C. Cleary, trans. *The Blue Cliff Record*. Boulder: Prajna Press, 1978.

Cook, Francis H., trans. *The Record of Transmitting the Light: Zen Master Keizan's Denkoroku*. Los Angeles: Center Publications, 1991.

Cook Francis H., trans. *Sounds of Valley Streams*. Albany: State University of New York Press, 1989.

Cook, Francis Dojun. *How to Raise an Ox*. Los Angeles: Center Publications, 1979.

Dogen, Eihei. "Shobogenzo Genjo Koan." Translated by Hakuyu Taizan Maezumi and Francis Cook. In *The Way of Everyday Life: Zen Master Dogen's Genjokoan*. Edited by Hakuyu Taizan Maezumi. Los Angeles: Center Publications, 1978.

Kapleau, Philip. *The Three Pillars of Zen: Teaching, Practice, and Enlightenment*. New York: Anchor, 1989.

Kim, Hee-Jin. *Dogen Kigen, Mystical Realist*. Tucson: University of Arizona Press, 1975.

Kim, Hee-Jin, trans. "Flowers of Emptiness: Selections from Dogen's Shobogenzo." *Studies in Asian Thought and Religion*. Vol. 2. Lewiston, NY: Edwin Mellen Press, 1985.

Maezumi, Hakuyu Taizan, ed. *The Way of Everyday Life: Zen Master Dogen's Genjokoan*. Los Angeles: Center Publications, 1978.

Maezumi, Hakuyu Taizan, and Bernard Tetsugen Glassman, eds. *On Zen Practice II: Body, Breath and Mind*. Los Angeles: Zen Center of Los Angeles, 1976.

Nishijima, Gudo, and Chodo Cross, trans. *Master Dogen's Shobogenzo*. London: Windbell Publications, 1996.

Nishiyama, Kosen, trans. *Shobogenzo*. Tokyo: Nakayama Shobo, 1983.

Tanahashi, Kazuaki, ed. *Moon in a Dewdrop: Writings of Zen Master Dogen*. San Francisco: North Point Press, 1985.

Waddell, Norman, and Masao Abe, trans. "Fukanzazengi: (The Universal Promotion of the Principles of Zazen) by Dogen Zenji." In *On Practice II: Body, Breath and Mind*, edited by Hakuyu Taizan Maezumi and Bernard Tetsugen Glassman. Los Angeles: Zen Center of Los Angeles, 1976.

Yamada, Koun. *The Gateless Gate*. 2nd ed. Tucson: University of Arizona Press, 1990.